A Tale of Two Journeys

A TALE OF TWO JOURNEYS

The Fry diaries: France & Belgium in the early 1800s

Joseph and Katharine Fry

Millrace

First published in Great Britain in 2005 by
Millrace
2a Leafield Road, Disley
Cheshire SK12 2JF
www.millracebooks.co.uk

ISBN: 1 902173 201

Typeset in Adobe Garamond Pro.
Printed and bound in the United Kingdom
by Cromwell Press Ltd, Trowbridge, Wiltshire.

Acknowledgements

Millrace would like to thank Richard C. Pelly for his help and co-operation in allowing these diaries to be published for the first time, for giving access to the Family Record compiled by Katharine Fry, and for suggesting the title of this book. Thanks, too, to the Library of the Religious Society of Friends in Britain for permission to reproduce the portrait of Joseph Fry by C. R. Leslie, J. Thomson's engraving of Elizabeth Fry, and Charlotte Giberne's drawing of the Fry children in 1830. All other illustrations are from the diaries themselves or the Family Record.

Most of the biographical material in the introductions and postscript comes from the Family Record, but June Rose's excellent biography of Elizabeth Fry (Macmillan, 1980) was also a valuable source of information and Jane Vansittart's selection of extracts from the Family Record (*Katharine Fry's Book*, Hodder & Stoughton, 1966) provided a vivid introduction to Fry family life.

Note

In transcribing Katharine Fry's 1874 fair copy of
these diaries, we have kept her spelling but altered
the punctuation to make the text easier to read.

Contents

Foreword

These diaries come from a book immaculately hand-written in the nineteenth century by my ancestor, Katharine Fry, daughter of the famous Quaker, Elizabeth. The book, which contains a fair copy of her father's and three of her own travel journals, has been carefully kept and passed from generation to generation, along with another that provides a meticulous record of the family history. These books nearly disappeared into America but were kept in England by a family arrangement that transferred them in 1922 to my great grandfather, Herbert Cecil Pelly, a direct descendant in the fourth generation of Joseph and Elizabeth Fry. They were subsequently bequeathed to me through my grandfather and father. The books are large (about 42cm by 25cm) and leather-bound, and have been kept in a special wooden box.

I became aware of their existence when my father brought them out to show visitors interested in their content. As a child, my eyes focused on the beautiful sketches. I could not read the script. It is only now during the preparation of this book that I have been able to read the transcript and discover that the descriptions of these journeys, which were undertaken about 200 years ago, are fascinating.

The travellers visited art and curiosity venues, just as we do today, but the additional feature is a sense of adventure inherent in such early tourism. The diarists comment on health, meals, the road, people met and, of course, the cost of things—again, just like today's travel writers. One of the people mentioned in the first journey took part in the Battle of Waterloo the following year.

I thank Millrace for transcribing these diaries into this book. We can now enjoy the content and wonder at the foresight of Katharine Fry, who began the book with a motto for collectors:

Things neither curious nor rare
May yet prove both if kept with care.

Richard Cecil Pelly
August 2005

Joseph Fry

In an age when women were expected to take second place to their menfolk, Joseph Fry is something of a rarity. Not only does he owe his place in history to his wife, but he gave her the backing and support that allowed her to carry out her remarkable work in prison reform. Although eclipsed by Elizabeth's fame, Joseph, as his travel diary shows, was a personality in his own right—shrewd, good humoured, observant. What is striking about the journal, written in 1814, is his eager, intelligent interest in his surroundings. To the disappointment of his daughter Katharine (and mirroring a criticism later made against Jane Austen, whose *Mansfield Park* was published that same year) Joseph does not focus on the momentous events of the period: it is the everyday experiences of the traveller that occupy and entertain him. He delights in personalities and landscapes, architecture and absurdities, and he records the minutiae of travel: the food, the prices, the fleas…

3

Joseph, the third son of a wealthy Quaker businessman, was born in 1777 in London's Cheapside, where the family tea firm was established. The house, in Bow Church Yard, had once been the Lord Mayor's mansion. Although business and family soon moved to St Mildred's Court, Joseph long remembered the magnificent painted ceilings (Juno and the peacocks was a particular favourite). This taste for the finer, more flamboyant things of life stayed with him, to the disapproval of some stricter Quakers. He loved music, too, as his daughter Katharine noted in the Family Record which she compiled in her old age:

> Our father had great facility in learning languages, and was a good French and Latin scholar. His decided preference however was for Music. He had a splendid voice and correct ear, but the prejudices of Quakerism forbad his receiving any instruction in it, and worse still made, by their positive prohibition of it, the simple exercise of his natural talent an act of disobedience and wrong doing. This had an injurious effect upon him and induced him occasionally to seek the indulgence of his taste and the exercise of his talent out of the family circle. He used to relate that when a boy at

4

school at Wandsworth, he wrote an Epithalamium
on the marriage of his cousin Esther Morris with
William Foster Reynolds, which was so well
approved that he was sent for to join the wedding
party, and at the Desert sang songs to them.

Joseph was not the only rebel in the family. His elder brother William was 'extremely fond of riding and driving and, notwithstanding his mercantile engagements in the City, became a scientific "whip"'. In fact, William seems to have been a better horseman than businessman. When he married in 1794, his father and mother retired to Plashet, their country estate, leaving their sons to take over the family firm. It extended into banking a few years later, with William running the bank, while Joseph managed the tea house. Over the next thirty years, William's rash loans and speculations led the firm into a series of financial crises.

Their middle brother, Thomas, died at the age of 26, but their younger sister—another Elizabeth— was always a close part of Joseph's own family life, and a friend and ally of his wife. As with William, her projects did not always prosper. Hearing of a young boy who had been brought to England from

Guinea, his parents having been murdered in the slave trade, she elected to take responsibility for him. He was sent to school, 'received a fair education, and became a humble member of the fireside circle at Plashet Cottage'. An attempt to put him into business proved disastrous: 'After being the means of losing nearly half her fortune, obliging her to lay down her carriage, &ca, it was necessary to get rid of him.' It was a sad story with a sad ending. He was sent to Liberia and there 'died in raving delirium of African fever, we believe somewhere about 1830'.

Joseph met and fell in love with Elizabeth Gurney on a visit to Earlham Hall, her family home near Norwich. It was the summer of 1798; he was 21, she 18. It took him some time to convince her (and her large, wealthy, well-connected Quaker family) that he was an acceptable suitor. She was not even sure that she should marry at all, However, he bore patiently with her wavering and, as she noted gratefully in her diary, 'behaved in the handsomest manner and said if I felt uneasy with the engagement, even an hour before the time of marriage, I was free to give it up.' His thoughtfulness shows in a postscript to a letter written shortly before their wedding:

I have got a certificate of marriage prepared &
have got the words 'affectionate' and 'faithful'
husband instead of loving as I thought thou would
like it better. Farewell my beloved.

They were married in August 1800. Elizabeth Fry's achievements later in life are now the stuff of history books but when she married, she was young and insecure. Her outbursts of worldliness were at odds with her beliefs and she worried about the direction her life should take. Joseph's love and admiration gave her the confidence and support she needed. When her vocation at last became clear, she was able, despite her numerous children, to follow it.

Early married life was not easy. Although William and his family moved out of St Mildred's Court, leaving the house for the newlyweds, they were rarely alone. Apart from the 'trade servants, twelve or fourteen in number' and business visitors, family members were always in and out, and there was a permanent flow of visiting Quakers. Elizabeth found the constant company stressful. In June 1801 she wrote in her diary: 'I do not think that since we married we have had one quarter of our meals alone. I *long* for more *retirement*.'

She was unhappy, too, that Joseph did not show as much zest for work as she thought proper (she had to get up early 'to get him to town in good time') and she feared he was a spendthrift. Once, when she scolded him for 'throwing away his money' on a caricature, he tore it in half and threw it on the fire—but soon had to be reproved for buying another drawing. The taste for acquiring art stayed with him: in 1825 he bought 'several Old Masters, including a portrait by Rembrandt and the interior of a church by Canaletto'. Some of Elizabeth's family were also concerned about his worldliness. After a financial crash many years later, her sister Rachel wrote:

> *How great a blessing for himself and others if he should be induced to make this a turning point and resolutely quit all those things that have proved great and dangerous snares to him, such as his love of music and the exercise of his magnificent voice which cannot in the view of Strict Friends be enjoyed even at home.*

Copying the letter into the Family Record, Katharine pointed out: 'My father was not of the strictest order of Friends, though he never questioned my Mother's beliefs.'

Joseph's other failings included an over-loud laugh and a fondness for chess, concerts and non-religious books. Nor was his natural ebullience always to Elizabeth's taste. On a trip north in 1801, Joseph 'was so exhilarated to be at the Lakes as to try my patience'. She thought Westmorland a dreary place, with 'too much lake and too much barren mountain'.

The situation grew much easier in 1809, after the death of Joseph's father, when they moved to Plashet, the family house in Essex. Elizabeth, who became a Minister not long afterwards, took her role as lady of the manor very seriously. Joseph enjoyed landscape gardening:

As soon as our father took possession of Plashet House, after the death of his father, he began to modernise the grounds. Landscape gardening was then in vogue. He therefore threw down the walls of the old garden, filled up the formal fish ponds and the Ha-Ha, cut down an avenue of Nut Trees, and worse still the grand Cherry Trees, of the size of forest trees, the pride of the gardens, for there were three gardens, distinct yet united...

They had three happy years at Plashet before the first of the business crises. Bankruptcy was avoided, thanks to the generosity of Elizabeth's family, but they were forced to economise by spending the winter at St Mildred's Court. It was while they were back in London that Elizabeth first became aware of the condition of women prisoners at Newgate. She at once set about organising working parties to make clothes for the prison babies, and persuaded the governor to allow her to visit the women. Although it was another three years before her work in prisons began in earnest, she was at last starting to understand where her energies and abilities should be directed.

This, then, was Joseph's home background when he made his trip to Belgium and France in October 1814, a few months after Elizabeth had given birth to their ninth child. In wider political and social terms, it was a significant period. In England, the Regency was three years old. Luddite riots were rumbling away in the north and, conscious of the appalling hardship in the country, Tory prime minister Lord Liverpool was doing his best to curb the Prince Regent's extravagances. Across the Channel, Napoleon Bonaparte's reign seemed to be over at last. Paris had fallen earlier that year, he was in exile on the island of Elba and Louis XVIII, brother of the guillotined king, was on the French throne. The following spring Napoleon escaped from Elba and returned briefly to power, only to be banished again after his defeat at Waterloo. It was during the first short period of his exile, with France once again opened up to English travellers after nearly twenty years of war, that Joseph set off to the Continent. With him were his nieces, Caroline and Eliza, and his own girls, Katharine and Rachel.

Leaving behind the pressures of business and family life, and a wife increasingly wrapped up in her work, Joseph Fry must have felt let off the leash. There is no indication that he was ever anything other than a devoted husband but the diary he kept on this holiday has a real air of anticipation and discovery.

> *The first entering a foreign place, was extremely singular & striking. Calais consists of houses, streets and squares, like towns in England, and yet in everything is unlike every town in England. The colours, & shape of the houses, the windows, the names & trades on the shops, the signs, numerous signs and devices, to say nothing of the people, give the feeling that you are in another land, not merely divided by a 'narrow frith'!*

Everything in Calais—their inn, their dinner, the

champagne and even the *vin ordinaire* ('very pleasant as a summer beverage, but it would be too tart for weak stomachs') is pleasing. Characteristically, Joseph instantly engages with the people he meets, the 'civil and pleasant Host', the 'modest' *fille de table*, the 'clever, diligent' Henri Duquesne, engaged as a servant for the tour. Even the 'irruption' of a bevy of forceful Englishwomen, ladies-in-waiting to the Duchess of Richmond, fails to disconcert him, though

> *I was most glad to escape from them, for we were all hungry, and our table just beautifully spread with glasses, napkins, rolls and waxlights, and in minutely expectation of our dinner, and then to have our seats occupied by the above mentioned resolute and appearantly ravenous ladies, would have been a trial, I should have ill stomached.*

As his daughter writes in a footnote, it was the same Duchess of Richmond whose ball on the eve of the Battle of Waterloo became so famous. Katharine is ever anxious to fill in the wider historical picture. When Joseph describes calling on Captain Gurwood, later editor of the 'Wellington Dispatches', she adds:

> *He does not mention that Captain Gurwood returned his visit one of the evenings, and sitting*

round the fire, we listened with breathless interest
to his recital of the storming of St Sebastian.

Again, at the end of the tour:

Our father omits to mention that at Boulogne we
saw rotting in the harbour, or rather on the mud
Banks, Buonoparte's famous fleet of flat bottomed
boats, intended for the invasion of England.

When Joseph does mention the war, it is only in
passing—as in his reference to crossing the Marne in
a boat because the bridge has been blown up—or to
the havoc the French have wrought in Belgium.

We went this morning to see the Cathedral, which
like all the fine churches here has been cruelly
robbed by the French, almost all the good pictures
carried to Paris, & even the very Churches put up
for sale & bought in by the inhabitants ... Indeed
wherever we have been, the french have left indel-
ible marks of their rapacity & want of feeling.

In Mons, too, he calls them 'modern Vandals' but his
opinion of France rises once he has crossed the bor-
der. He finds a 'capital' bookseller in Cambrai and
the Soleil d'Or at Royes proves 'the cleanest house &
nicest in every way we had met with in France; we
had sheets both clean and dry, & for a wonder *clean*

13

floors.' Though an exorbitant price for a meal with a 'bottle of vile wine' at Chapell en Servac is a setback, Joseph is soon firmly under France's spell:

> *...the open airy effect produced from the entire absence of enclosure of any kind, joined to the extensive views & feeling of expance every where, is charming & almost exhilarating. I could not help often repeating to myself, 'possessed of France what can the French wish for more!'*

His appreciation of the countryside is clear from the time they leave Calais. As the carriage rolls through Belgium, its passengers amused by the dexterity with which the postillions flourish their whips, Joseph notes landscape and architecture, the neatness and decency of the villages and farms, the 'few neat tall Chateaux', the cottages 'painted with a reddish ochre with a good deal of dark green about them' and the general air of cleanliness and comfort. It is, he decides, 'superior even to our beloved England'.

Paris is even more irresistible. Equipped with a velvet bonnet, which he is endearingly convinced makes him look 'completely *french*', he packs in an astonishing amount of sightseeing, visiting and dining out while he is in the city—and thrives on it:

I cannot help liking Paris. I am getting to feel very much at home here. One thing I have no doubt has more effect than I am aware of, which is, that the air & diet, & even water (filtered) unquestionably agree with me better than those of England, & I awake in a morning more refreshed & freer from headaches. NB. I think I have once or twice felt a flea, in the day time, since I came to Paris, a week tomorrow—but except that, I have neither seen or felt any species of Vermin.

As always, he observes his fellow men. He thoroughly approves of the way in which the people are allowed right into the palace yard: 'In Paris every thing is done to please and make happy the common people. In England their feelings are too much disregarded.' One evening, accompanied by his *valet de place*, he sallies forth to the Palais Royal, visiting the underground cafés and observing a celebrated beauty seated in a railed box. And he mingles with the crowds at the Jardin des Plantes, marvelling at the menagerie of Wild Beasts and the Amphitheatre of Anatomy, 'a most curious collection, consisting of Mummies from Egypt & Teneriffe, also various other human specimens & monstrosities...'

He even finds time to take a warm bath at the Bains Virgier with a 'hand-basin full of highly perfumed soap froth'. Only the advent of Sunday halts the spate of outings. 'We kept quietly at home the whole day, & in the forenoon read part of the Ephesians, & sat after it, I hope not unsatisfactorily. It was very dull work to be shut in all day.'

But, for Joseph, nothing is dull work for long. When the time comes to leave Paris, he puts aside his regrets and, with characteristic gusto and adaptability, sets about extracting maximum enjoyment from the journey home.

At Airaines, not having time to alight for refreshment, I procured a bottle of wine which we drank off, & I got some excellent slices from a gigot de mouton roti, dressed as in England, & put it on a plate with some salt & slices of bread, & paying the charge, & placing it on our knees in the carriage, drove off in excellent humour...

Trip to Belgium and Paris, 1814
by Joseph Fry

The journey of which the following journal is a record was made by our father in the autumn of the year 1814. He was accompanied by his two nieces, Caroline and Eliza Fry, and daughters Katharine and Rachel. The two latter were too young to estimate the great interest of such a visit to Paris, at such an historical period, but some vivid recollections of it are still (1874) retained by both of them. With the exception of the short peace of Amiens in 1802, France and the greater part of the Continent had been closed to Englishmen since 1793, in consequence of the wars subsequent to the great French Revolution. It may be supposed, therefore, with what eager curiosity the scenes of such stiring events were visited; and how strange every thing in France and Belgium appeared to English eyes.

The style of the journal is meagre: very much of great interest slightly touched upon, or altogether passed over; but there is enough to render it (in my opinion) worth copying into this book.

'Things neither curious nor rare
May yet prove both if kept with care.'

It is now sixty years ago since it was written, and great changes have since taken place, which render even meagre accounts of the manners, mode of travelling and appearance of the country worth preserving.

Katharine Fry, November 1874

Dunkirk, 6th day,[1] 10th mo 7. 1814

I arrived at Dover on the morning the 6th of 10th mo., 1814, accompanied by my nieces Caroline and Eliza, and my Katharine and Rachel, with Thomas Hardwick.[2] The York Hotel is a poor house, and more exorbitant for middling fare than any house I have ever yet been at, for the best accommodation. We paid 2s/6d each for breakfast of execrable tea and rolls and butter. After many delays we set sail[3] at 2 o'clock & by 10 minutes past five were safely moored by Calais pier, which is very long & forms with a bank on the opposite side a good harbour, like a river. Swarms of Frenchmen & children were on the quay to see us arrive, & in a minute a dozen were leaping into our vessel to offer their services, untill they were requested to retire. 'Donnez-moi un sous, Monsieur,'

[1] *For Quakers, Sunday was known as First day, Monday, Second day, etc.*
[2] *KF: His coachman. (These footnotes are provided by Katharine Fry.)*
[3] *KF: Our father hired a sloop, a little yatcht-like thing, which conveyed us and our carriage. She was called 'The Defence'. The price was £5.*

was exclaimed, & ten times repeated, by a little fellow about 12 years old; & on landing all crowded round offering their services to conduct us to the Hotels, each of which had their people waiting.

The first entering a foreign place was extremely singular & striking. Calais consists of houses, streets and squares, like towns in England, and yet in every thing is unlike every town in England. The colours, & shape of the houses, the windows, the names & trades on the shops, the signs, numerous signs and devices, to say nothing of the people, give the feeling that you are in another land, not merely divided by a 'narrow frith'!

We found Quillacque, who with Duplessis keeps Dessin's Hotel, a remarkably civil and pleasant Host. Although his own house was full, and could not lodge us, yet he placed us comfortably at a little Inn in 'Rue du Soleil', kept by one St Louis, who with his wife and daughter did all in their power to make us comfortable. We dined at Dessin's, with the Messers, our companions for the day.[1]

[1] KF: The Messers: the sons of a very leading London Friends' family. Their sister, Hannah Messer, was one of twelve original Newgate Committee with our mother.

Whilst the table was preparing, we were considerably disturbed by the irruption of 4 or 5 smart looking females, who entered exclaiming, 'This is the room, we were to have' & shewing a great inclination to despute our possession. I went to the one who seemed the principal, and who seemed a person of some importance, at least equal to a Banker's wife, & was modestly going to inform her, I feared there was some mistake, and to offer to withdraw with my party, when two of the ladies hastily drew chairs to the table, and were clapping themselves into them, to ensure their right, with a manner & resolution that I should not have ventured to oppose, when luckily for me, one of the principals of the House came into the room, and assured the ladies that another room was ready for them, and that the one we were disputing was for me and my party. I had heard that the Duchess of Richmond[1] was in the house, but I little dreamt that I should have such a roncontre with no less persons than 4 or 5 of her Grace's waiting maids, I mean ladies in waiting! I was most glad to escape

[1]KF: *This lady's ball at Brussels, in the following June, on the eve of the Battle of Waterloo, has become historical. She was on her way to Brussels when we encountered her suite at Calais.*

from them, for we were all hungry, and our table just beautifully spread with glasses, napkins, rolls and waxlights, and in minutely expectation of our dinner, and then to have our seats occupied by the above mentioned resolute and appearantly ravenous ladies, would have been a trial I should have ill stomached.

Our dinner was excellent. Potage au vermiceil, fricandeau à l'oreille, Beefstake and un volaille roti were the chief, & some excellent champagne. I tasted the vin ordinaire blanc, & found it very pleasant as a summer beverage, but it would be too tart for weak stomachs.

We retired after dinner to St Louis's and found a cheerful room and a good wood fire in an open fire place, and coffee was served in beautiful porcelain, & tea offered. Our rooms were dull looking and peculiar, the papers smart and like Indian paper, but a part of the rooms dark inlaid wainscot, & the ceilings painted dark colours. The doors and window fixtures, & all the iron work and fastenings, were old fashioned & of very clumsey, indifferent workmanship, a hundred years behind us at least. Our beds were hard, but clean, and no vermin or closeness.

The 'fille de chambre', Theresa, was a good natured

cheerful girl, and the 'fille de table', Mlle Nouville de St Louis, was a fine french face & a sweet modest young woman; in short, the whole family pleased me. At parting, the latter girl asked for nothing, but I told her father I wished to remember her. 'Vous étés trop bon Monsieur' was his reply; however, I prevailed on her to accept 2½ francs.

And now I must give Calais a character. I saw it by day and walked out at night with the Messers; it was then more quiet than most English towns & I neither saw nor heard, all the time I was there, one thing offensive to decency or good morals.

Having parted with Thomas, before I left the place I engaged as a servant for our tour, Henri Duquesne, a decent, middle aged man. He speaks French, Flemish and German. I engaged him for 8 francs per diem, to find himself, every thing, and I have reason so far to be satisfied with my choice; he seems clever, diligent, and faithful.

After furnishing myself with a velvet bonnet, like a Highlander's in shape, and very generally in use for travellers, we left Calais, drawn by 4 horses, and 2 postilions. I was struck with the appearance of the Church yards. At the head of every tomb, a little black, or black and white, wooden cross gives them a most singular and rather grotesque appearance.

The road from Calais to Dunkirk lies through Gravelines, a fortress once of prodigeous strength, but fast falling to decay. The whole country is flat & uninteresting, a good deal like the fen country about the Isle of Ely. The road [is] nearly perfectly straight through rows of Willows and Hornbeams, closely planted.

From the general tenor of the conversation I have had with the french hitherto, both civil and military, I should judge them much satisfied with their new government, and also their opinions are favorable to a continuance of peace.

Dunkirk is a good town and an excellent harbour and quay, but much fallen off in its population & general prosperity. The weather being cool, my young companions ventured abroad in their Plaids, but were so rudely assailed by a multitude of children,[1] that we were glad to get into our Inn, the Hotel d'Angleterre, to be out of the way. The apartments and fare here are very agreeable, & if our beds trim and comfortable as

[1] *KF: It was rude curiosity, our plaids were taken as a proof that we were connected with the Highland Regiments, of whose valor prodigies were told.*

they look, we shall have no cause to complain. NB
We have carefully read the scriptures both mornings.

Bruges, 7th day, 10th mo 8. 1814
After a good night to all parties, except myself who
had far too intimate an intercourse with an enormous
flea to have uninterrupted rest, we rose, breakfasted,
paid our bill at the Hotel d'Angleterre. For a capital
dinner, coffee, lodging and breakfast, the charge was
51 francs 10 cen., with an addition of 3 fr.10 to the
waiter and chambermaid, or about in all £2.6s.
    After a slight examination at the Barrier (in which
we fared much better than the Duchess of Richmond,
who was detained on the Quay for an hour and a half,
and was obliged in consequence to sleep at Ghistelles,
a very small place, instead of getting on to Bruges) we
proceeded about 9 miles on a fine beach, covered with
uncommon quantities of shells, to Tapanne, a miserable range of 2 or 3 Huts, just after passing a large
board, written upon 'Extrème Frontière Belgique', &
on arriving were stopped by a Hanoverian Douanier,
who civilly demanded to see our Baggage. Duquesne
told him we were des voyageurs anglais & assured
him we had no contraband with us, and supposed he

wanted 'un pièce'. He said no, he wished for nothing, but at last consented to take our word, and a franc, & suffered us to pass on unmolested; nine miles further to Furnes.

Through a very dull, flat country, with scarce a tree, except a few stunted Willows and Alder, but well sprinkled with decent villages and farms. Here we had to wait an hour for horses, at a small Inn, the 'Poste au Chevaux', and again had to fee a Hanoverian douanier with a franc, for forebearing to turn out every package, even to our nightclothes, into the street.

We next proceeded to Ghistelles, about 19 miles through a country a little more inland, & rather more enclosed, but from Dunkirk to Bruges, a distance of near 50 miles, I have not seen an elevation half as high as that from Bow Bridge to Bow Church, or even from Elizabeth's fosse to her cottage: it is one uniform, perfect level, & for nearly half the way, with scarcely a hedge or a tree. Ghistelles is a small town with nothing remarkable but the ruins of a pretty, large old Chateau, formerly moated.

We next proceeded on towards Bruges, amused from time to time, as on our whole journey, by the

loud clacking of the Postilions' whips, which they do with surprising dexterity, whirling them round their heads, and cracking them over the right and left shoulders alternately, with a very loud noise which may be heard to a considerable distance.

Between Ghistelles and this place (Bruges) the country much improves in beauty & culture: a pretty deal of small wood, but none fine or well grown. We were delayed by a curious accident on our road. About half way from Ghistelles, we suddenly came to a full stop at a broken bridge, and I soon heard a loud altercation between Duquesne & a party of men who were working at the bridge. The conversation was in broad flemish, but from the gestures and some of the expressions, I judged that very high words were passing. I soon descended from the carriage and found that the right of the cause was certainly with my man. As these flemish wiseacres had taken up about three or four yards in length of the planks of the bridge, & as they were employed by authority in mending it, they seemed to have no idea of any alternative but our staying there, till the bridge was repaired. However, as my man's rhetoric was too violent to obtain his end, I tryed soft words to one, who understood french, & soon prevailed. 'Vous étés brave,' said the man, 'mais quant à cet homme là, il parle comme s'il eut eté un Baron!' & immediately with the help of the postillions laid down about 10 planks, over which the carriage was safely conveyed.

I have noticed in coming through Flanders several small chapels, about four to five feet square, by the road side, with a small portico in front and a bench to kneel on, opposite to a small grate, within which is placed some crucifix, or image of the Virgin. I examined one and found the inside dressed up like a puppet show, with a figure of the Virgin like rather an ordinary wax, or leather doll, with a smaller doll in her arms. Nothing but respect to the religious prejudices of those in our company who were catholics, would have prevented me from a fit of laughter at the ludicrous scene the whole thing presented. Though perhaps weeping would have been at least as appropriate. I have also been disgusted several times today with the sight of large crucifixes against the Churches, with figures of our Saviour as large as life and painted to imitate flesh. I believe we know better, but I have been truly pleased with the apparent simplicity and honesty of the Flemish people who worship in this way.

Bruges is a large, fine old city; the houses like many in Flanders are very ancient & shew that the place was once opulent and flourishing. The Cathedral, the StadHouse, Maison du Prefecture & many of the private houses are handsome edifices. The Cathedral is, to me, not a very fine edifice. We lodged at the 'Fleur de Blé', a large Inn but a large, rambling mis-shapen place, but the house and articles were clean and the provisions good. I have the pleasure to repeat my declaration of yesterday, that (with the exception of a few vulgar exclamations & oaths, certainly not to a greater degree than in England) I have as yet met with nothing contrary to decency or good manners.

Bruges Bill 37 fr. 10. Ghent 68 fr. 85 c.

Ghent, 1st day, 10th mo 9. 1814
We travelled this day from Bruges, about 30 miles, through a country continually flat, but much diversi-fied with woods, some of tollerable growth, & sprin-kled with a few neat, tall Chateaux, with gardens all

laid out in the old fashioned style, and abundance of villages & farms, wearing together with their inhabitants neatly attired in their Sunday clothes, a most cheerful & picturesque appearance. Scores of them took off their hats, or touched them, & they looked upon us with apparent kindness in their hearts. In particular I was struck with the beauty of the village of Boissieu, between Ecloo and Ghent. The cottages were of a long shape, & rather like short rows of cottages than a single one, having mostly only the ground floor. Some of them were painted with a reddish ochre, with a good deal of dark green about them—and dark green doors and windows on a white ground. The air of cleanliness & comfort that pervaded every thing was certainly quite superior even to our beloved England.

Most of the roads in Flanders are edged with trees, & from Bruges to Ghent almost the whole way, with pretty fine grown beech, trimmed up about 20 feet, with strait stems and bushy tops, along roads that for miles together are perfectly straight & form a perspective so accurate as only to terminate in a speck. Without the deviation of one tree from the straight line, [it] formed a novel and highly beautiful scene,

& different from anything I ever have met with. In short, this part of Brabant is a perfect garden, rich, fertile, covered with wood & underwood, a smiling country & a happy population. I asked several of them how they liked their seperation from France. A smile of unaffected pleasure left me no doubt as to the truth of the declaration that they were rejoiced at the change. But I have not yet asked any question pointedly as to their feeling about union with Holland. But I have found the English much liked, particularly as I have advanced more inland.

The approach to Ghent is very striking: the road runs for miles along the banks of a very wide canal, much broader than the river Lea and perfectly straight, & at the termination one sees the beautiful towers of the fine Cathedral & Churches, Ghent rising to view in the distance. The effect is like two roads, one by land & one by water, intersperced with carts, foot passengers, & neat barges running parallel and straight, & terminating in the lofty edifices of the city rising in majesty in the distance.

Ghent is a fine, large city, & like Fernnes, Bruges and many other Flemish towns, has great numbers of houses built in a very peculiar manner in the Spanish taste, with the front rising to a peak, like steps up each side, only very tall, and many ornamented thus:

It is a cheerful town, and a respectable, well dressed population. In short, were I choose a country after England, I think it would be the Netherlands. The chimes here are half hourly, and the most beautiful and different from any I ever heard elsewhere.

Brussels, 2nd day, 10th mo 10. 1814

We went this morning to view the fine Cathedral at Ghent which for beauty and magnificence, and the fine statuary & some good paintings it contains, far exceeds anything in England. A standing figure of Christ in marble of exquisite workmanship, another of Christ being scourged, & recumbent statues of several Bishops of Ghent would at least repay a journey to view them, at least if the Sea was not between.

It is impossible for me to convey an idea of the splendour and richness of the decorations, the Altar, the candlesticks, the gildings, the variety of marbles, and the whole brilliant and dazzling effect of this most sumptuous edifice. I could not longer wonder at the veneration of the Catholics, when every thing is contrived to overpower the sober reasoning faculty & awe the imagination.

From Ghent we came by Alost, 42 miles to Brussels, through a charming country, and for the last 20 miles considerably diversified by a fine but gentle undulation in the surface of the country.

Brussels is a large populous trading town, & the upper part, namely the Park and adjoining houses & streets, are very handsome & airy. The Park is small as a park, but very large and beautiful as a square, full of good trees in avenues & surrounded by fine houses, built in a handsome style. We are at the Hotel d'Angleterre, a good house, but very inferior to one or two in the place, which are very full.

I called on Captain Gurwood,[1] aid de camp to

---

[1]KF: *It is remarkable how little notice our father seems to have taken of the important historical fact of the British Army being quartered in Brussels and the surrounding district. He does not mention that Captain Gurwood returned his visit one of the evenings, and sitting round the fire, we listened with breathless interest to his recital of the storming of St Sebastian—being himself one of those who led the storming parties to the Breach. As Colonel Gurwood, he was well known as the Editor of the 'Wellington Dispatches'. Our acquaintance with him was only this one occasion at Brussels. The Battle of Waterloo was fought the 28th June following.*

General Clinton here, but unluckily found him going out tomorrow with his Hussars to Alost; he behaved very politely and agreeably. We propose resting here tomorrow. (Bill for 1st day 57 frs.)

Brussels, 3rd day, 10th mo 11. 1814
We went this morning to see the Cathedral, which like all the fine churches here has been cruelly robbed by the French, almost all the good pictures carried to Paris, & even the very Churches put up for sale & bought in by the inhabitants. In the Cathedral here, pavement was considerably injured by the trampling of Horses, as I myself saw. And but for the beautiful stained glass windows being carefully hid, that striking beauty of this cathedral would have been demolished. As it is, the effect of the colored glass, of which about six large windows are composed, is very striking and beautiful. We also saw the Chapelle Sabloniere, a fine church dedicated to the Virgin, and the Museum in which very few good pictures remain, & the Natural curiosities have also been robbed without mercy. Indeed, wherever we have been, the french have left indelible marks of their rapacity & want of feeling.

We next went to see the Palace of Laken, formerly the residence of the Archduke Albert.[1] The house on the outside appears out of repair, but within is in the highest order, & the grounds are delightful. It is the best instance I know of the happy mixture of utility and state. We went about in a hired carriage for which we paid 10 francs, with a Valet de Place named Vincent, who knew french but indifferently & not much of anything. We returned home to an excellent dinner at 5 o'clock, of which out of many dishes, some were intelligible, particularly a good piece 'du Rosbeef' & a coliflower, neither of them overdressed.

Paris, 6th day, 10th mo 14. 1814
We left Brussels early on 4th day and breakfasted at Hal, a small town about 12 miles from Brussels, & afterwards proceeded to Mons, where we paid a visit to a Convent of Ursuline Nuns. We rung a small bell near a little grating, closed by an oaken partition, which was presently opened by a sweet looking

[1]KF: *This relates to the period of the Austrian possession of this part of the Netherlands, previous to the french revolution, and the absorption of ye Netherlands by France.*

elderly nun, who gave us a key which opened into a large parlour, one side of which was grated off from another small room, into which soon after came a fat, proud & rather illnatured looking nun, the Abbess of the Convent, who seeing my party of young girls, thought I came to leave them as boarders, and assured me she had no room. I assured her they would be *terribly frightened* if I was to leave them there, & by dint of good humour on my part, brought her into it too. She offered me to go into the Church, which I accepted: a small but beautiful building, opening lengthways into the Convent, and having partitions seperating it from a sort of side aisle or chapel in which the Nuns were assembled. We could hear them chanting a sort of prayer, and on listening was struck with hearing them put up a petition 'pour les voyageurs anglais'. The whole effect was striking, and produced a pleasing melancholy, so far as I could believe them accepted, in their sincerity.

The Cathedral at Mons is a fine edifice, but not equal to some we had seen. It showed indelible marks of the ravages of the modern Vandals, several beautiful marble railings being carried away & sold, of which one specimen left is sufficient proof. It also possesses two or three small, good paintings by Vandyke and Rubens. The numerous grotesque figures of the Virgin dressed in every fantastic form of clothing, & bedecked with lace & trumpery, are a melancholy spectacle.

We slept at the 'Grand Canard' at Valencennes, where we had pretty good entertainment & a bill of 52 fr. We were waited upon here by a Garçon de Table named Antoine Dubois, whose drollery of manner & extreme officiousness were ludicrous beyond description. He entertained us at our meals with abundance of conversation on various subjects. Luckily for us, by occasionally leaving the room he left an opening for laughter, which it was almost impossible to suppress. When he had put on our Desert, in particular, he amused us by a most unexpected sally; he had put on the last dish when, drawing himself up quite straight & throwing his head back & clapping his arms to his sides à la militaire, exclaimed, 'Voila Monsieur ce que je viens de vous presenter'!!

We breakfasted at the public table, in company with two french officers, one of them wearing the cross of St Louis, who were tolerably pleasant company. We reached Cambray about ½ past 3 o'clock,

& I went directly to Hurzez the Bookseller in a large capital shop. He was so obliging as to accompany us to the Tomb and Palace of Fenelon. What is called the Tomb is a narrow oak coffin of the usual length, with the top sloping like the roof of a house, in which carefully sealed up and attested lie the bones of that truly pious Christian Bishop. It is covered with a blue silk & surrounded by several pieces of statuary and the remainder of the broken tombstone, with his name very legible.

The palace and old cathedral are in ruins. The present cathedral is possessed of much beauty, and some invaluable works of art. It has one fine painting by Rubens, but its chief ornaments are 8 paintings in stone colors by Geeraeres of Antwerp, which for effect of relief surpass any paintings I ever saw. They actually appeared to start from the canvas, & so complete was the illusion, that I could not be satisfied they were mere paintings, untill I took an opportunity of a close inspection, so as to ascertain that the wall was actually level.

We slept this night at Royes, where L. & M. Schimmelpenick complained of every thing being so uncomfortable, but with us the reverse was the case;

we were at the 'Soleil d'or'. They charged pretty high, 52 fr, but it was the cleanest house & nicest in every way we had met with in France; we had sheets both clean and dry, & for a wonder *clean floors*. We set off after an early breakfast & reached this place, Paris, about ½ past 6 o'clock, to excellent apartments at the 'Hotel de l'Empire'.

The country we passed through has been generally fine and well cultivated. From Brussels, for the first 40 miles, a fine covered country, with easy swells in the land. From thence to Royes, considerably naked, & from Royes to Paris, more and more enclosed, rich and wooded, & for miles from the other side Senlis to Paris, very thickly wooded, & beautiful in many parts.[1] The general appearance of france is delightful, & the open airy effect produced from the entire absence of enclosure of any kind, joined to the extensive views & feeling of expance every where, is

[1] KF: *Senlis is surrounded by three great forests, those of Chantilly, Halatte and Ermenonville; our father might call the district 'wooded thickly'. It was towards dark on this day that we were startled by the Claquée of our postillions' whips and their shouts of 'au loup! au loup!' We distinctly saw two wolves run across the road a little way before us, into the Forest. In 1837, travelling also with my father through the forest of Cerecy in Normandy, between St Lo & Bayeux, we again saw a wolf run across the road before our carriage, in the dusk of an autumn afternoon.*

charming & almost exhilarating. I could not help often repeating to myself, 'possessed of France what can the French wish for more!'

We have throughout experienced more civility & kindness and less impertinent curiosity in France than in the Netherlands, but from stage to stage have been pestered with Beggars of all sorts and sizes, and numerous attempts at imposition, in which we found our french servant eminently serviceable.

Today we crossed the Marne at Pont de M. in a ferry boat, the fine stone bridge having been blown up on account of the allies. At Chapelle en Servac we stopped at a small place 22 miles from Paris, to take a chop (cotelete). They produced us a cold chicken, a tolerable plenty of good mutton chops, with some sour bread, & a bottle of vile wine; for which the honest landlady asked us 20 francs. I only got off by paying 15. The only way with these people is to make your bargain before hand, or you can hardly escape from their rapacity.

The apartments here are very handsome, but dear. I have engaged them at a week certain for 15 Louis, or if two weeks at 27 Louis, & to have furniture and linen found. All the rest we pay for.

Paris, 1st day, 10th mo 16. 1814

After calling on Faber (the Banker) who was extremely kind, we began our operations here in a voiture de remise, and after several vain attempts to buy some cheap silks we drove to the Jardin des Plantes. In our way we stopped in front of the Thuilleries, before the fine triumphal arch erected by Napoleon; the design & execution were both superb, & the brazen Horses, which were brought from the Place St Marc at Venice, by Lycippus, on the top are equal to every encomium that has been bestowed on them.

We were lucky enough just at this moment to see two of the King's coaches with 8 horses (himself being in one of them), with a party of Guards, drive off from the Palace gate. The outside of this palace, and of the Louvre, are more than equal to my expectations. They are truly Royal, and the familiar way the people were admitted into the palace yard, up to the very door, occasioned me to draw an unfavorable comparison between this Court and that of Carlton House. In Paris every thing is done to please and make happy the common people. In England their feelings are too much disregarded.

I felt the difference forcibly in that part of the

Jardin des Plantes where the menagerie of Wild Beasts is situated. Unlike ours in the Tower, they are so placed that over a railing about 4 feet high, any body who pleases can see that fine collection of animals at a distance of about 5 feet from their dens. I remarked a circumstance which I have no doubt is a consequence of the continual access of the public, which was that the animals seem to have lost their ferocity in a greater degree than I have before noticed any where, & at the same time the public at all times enjoy the innocent pleasure of beholding a sight, always more or less interesting. In particular, several deep paved courts of considerable size, into which you look over a parapet, where several bears are kept, with a tree in the middle of each for them to climb up, form a source of constant entertainment to the Parisians.

They are also admitted to a part of the Jardin des Plantes, through which are broad walks in every direction, edged with trees, and seats at intervals. The plants are inclosed in parterres, in rows labeled, & can be seen by every one, over a slight fence of lattice work. Adjoining the gardens are various enclosures for different sorts of animals: Elephants, Dromedaries, varieties of Deer, of Birds, &ca—a great variety. Many of these are also accessible to the public. Also adjoining this collection is the amphitheatre of Anatomy, a most curious collection, consisting of Mummies from Egypt & Teneriffe, also various other human specimens & monstrosities of all kinds, an astonishing number. Among other objects, I noticed the skeleton of the Camelopardalis, & the skin of a Human head with the hair and beard on, dressed into leather, of not much less thickness than that of a sheep, skeletons of Men, Beasts, Birds, Fishes & Serpents, admirably disposed and arranged, together with a great variety of surgical curiosities.

From this place we went to the Upper end of the garden, to the 'Cabinet de l'histoire naturelle'. It consists of two very long galleries, one above the other; in the lower are a countless variety of specimens of minerals and fossils of all descriptions, together with fishes, lizards & serpents. In the higher (gallery) are other animals, but above all of Birds, shells & insects, all scientifically classed, & forming in the whole a collection which must be now unrivalled in the world, & untill irrisistible Time destroys it, in my opinion will always remain so. It must be seen to

43

be appreciated, & to be at all well described would require great abilities & a thorough knowledge of natural history in all its branches. In short, it excited astonishment & admiration, which recur every time I think of this most marvellous assemblage of the wonders and beauties of Nature!

In the evening I put on my french velvet 'bonnet', which though so plain, made me look completely *french,* and buttoning my great coat I sallied forth, attended by Bourdon, our valet de Place, who is really an intelligent steady fellow, & determined to see as much as I could of the interior of the Palais Royal, of which I had heard so much. I accordingly began at one part & went on till I came round to the same place again.

It forms a very large oblong square, the interior of which is pleasantly laid out as a garden, with walks, and parterres, & a great number of seats of various kinds, & like all things here, always open to the public. Round all the sides of this square, and in several parallel rows and entrance passages, are all sorts of shops, containing wherewith to satisfy every imaginable want, glittering with profusion of lights, & thronged with all sorts of people, chiefly those who are persuing in various ways the idol of the Parisians, pleasure. In the one pair are gaming & other houses of all sorts but *Good* purposes.

In passing along, my guide called my attention to a winding staircase, down which I went & found myself in the 'Café des Aveugles', a large room, or rather cluster of rooms opening promiscuously into each other, all brilliantly lighted, the busy scene within reflected by numbers of looking glasses. The space was covered with tables, at which sat numbers of cheerful countenances of both sexes, some drinking beer, others lemonade, or what they pleased, & at intervals had music and a species of farce to amuse them.

From there we went to the 'Café Montansier', anciently the Theatre Montansier; the figure and general appearance of a theatre are still maintained. Shrubs and flowers were placed in different parts, and from the ground floor up to the second story, and in all the ranges of seats on each story and the whole of the wide staircase, swarms of people of all descriptions, but generally well dressed, are to be seen throughout the whole evening. All sorts of refreshments are served on numerous tables to those who desire them.

Besides these I visited three more underground cafés, a good deal similar to the Café des Aveugles. Namely, 'Le Café du Caveau', 'Du Sauvage' & 'Des Varietés'. In two of which I heard really fine music & singing. In another, called the 'Café des Milles Colonnes', in a railed box serving those who take any refreshment, sits the celebrated beauty Madame Romain, who is considered the finest woman in Paris, decked out in profuse gaiety of dress and sitting to be looked at. From this novel scene I returned fatigued home.

This day (1st day, 10th mo 16) we kept quietly at home the whole day, & in the forenoon read part of the Ephesians, & sat after it, I hope not unsatisfactorily. It was very dull work to be shut in all day, but our efforts to get our people to a place of worship seemed in vain. In the evening we took a coach and went to ride out for a little air, & to see the state of things so much talked of, on a first day evening. Along the Boulevards were crowds of people, & the shops lighted up with unusual splendour. The Boulevard du Temple was like a Fair. Theatres, shows & mountebanks, music & dancing, buying & selling. All sorts of people except the most respectable classes formed

Paris fashions in winter 1814-1815, from a rough sketch by D. Gurney

the company, & this for the evening of that day by us English set apart for Services & Observances. The accounts I had heard were in all respects true to their fullest extent. I observed in passing along the 'Café des Princes', a place which has a brilliant & very light centre to attract, but on each side are sombre, and even dark alleys, & numerous recesses with seats for those who like to use them, for drinking or conversation. The Chateau d'Eau is a large curious Hydraulic fountain, & in summer must spread a grateful coolness in its vicinity, but its height appeared to me very disproportionate to its great circumference, which must be 120 yards at least.

Paris, 2nd day, 10th mo 17. 1814
This morning I learnt with some dismay that the Louvre was about to be closed to every one in 2 days, & that even at present strangers are only admitted by tickets, & no french people. I sent off to Baron Denon to request a ticket of admission, and received one for this day, & tomorrow, but on attempting to see the statues were disappointed, but we hope to succeed tomorrow. We spent several hours, however, in viewing the astonishing collection of paintings, which I shall not attempt to describe, as neither my time, or abilities are sufficient. I may say of it, as of the Cabinet of Natural History, that it clearly showed itself to be the assembled spoils of Europe.

From the Louvre we walked in the gardens of the Thuilleries, in which we saw evidently many very fashionable people, and afterwards took a delightful

drive through the Champs Elysées & past the triumphal arch, which Bonaparte began, but which now
preaches a sermon to all Kings & all their subjects,
to the Bois de Boulogne. We returned by the Place
Vendome, past the astonishing column erected by
Bonaparte, of the metal of the cannon taken from
Austria, and on getting home were agreeably surprised to find Charles Buxton's[1] card on our man-
telpiece. After dinner we all went over to the Hotel
D'Autriche to call on him & Martha & Amelia. It
was truly pleasant to see them again, & we expect to
see them again tomorrow, to dinner at our Hotel.

Paris, 3rd day, 10th mo 18. 1814
This morning we renewed our attempt to see the statues of the Louvre, in which by the help of an order
from Baron Denon, we luckily succeeded & spent
several hours in this astonishing assemblage. My first
sensations were delightful, but almost overpowering.
I thought that once got in, I should be hard to force
out until I had enjoyed the full satisfaction of survey-
ing the whole. After several hours we again went for a

[1]KF: *Brother of the first Baronet. His widow was afterwards Mrs Carr.
Martha & Amelia were his wife & her sister Amelia Henning.*

short time to the paintings, & from thence returned home very much fatigued. After this day the Louvre closes till the 1st of next month; so that luckily we were just in time to see it before it was too late.[1]

Paris, 4th day, 10th mo 19. 1814
We set off this morning & saw the beautiful, ancient Cathedral of Notre Dame. Its stained glass is very fine, and it has some good paintings by french artists, but its most striking work of art is a series of 16 or 18 bas reliefs in black oak, containing some of the more striking circumstances connected with the birth & life of our Saviour. In a room in the building we were shown the robes & regalia, also the canopy of the Pope, the embroidered vestments of the Priests, used at the Coronation of Bonaparte, also the regalia, spurs &ca of Charlemagne, with some relics, & amongst them a gilt globe *said* to contain the real crown of thorns, worn by our Saviour, but as it was not opened, I had no opportunity of judging of its antiquity.

[1] *KF: Although sixty years have passed, the Venus de Medeci, the Lyacoon, and above all the Apollo of Belvedere remain graven in my mind. November, 1874.*

We next saw St. Sulpice, and from thence to the Petits Augustins, to see the ancient monuments of France which have been rescued by Le Noir from revolutionary frenzy. They begin some of them at the Xtian era, & come down to the present time. I was interested, amongst others, with the tomb of Abelard & Eloisa.

Lastly we saw the Grand & Petit Luxembourg, which contains chiefly an interesting set of fine paintings by Le Sueur, comprising the History of St. Bruno, & the foundation of the Grand Chartreuse. Next, a gallery of large & fine paintings by Rhubens, containing allegorical representations of the principal events of the life of Mary de Medicis. And next a charming set of views in the Gallery of Vernet of the chief ports of France, both military & commercial. We then descended in order to see the Hall of the Senate, & as we had a short time to wait, a gentleman of most pleasing manners invited us to follow him & took us up a long back staircase to a private entrance; he then ordered somebody to bring him his key, and opening the door gave orders to some of the officers to shew us into the rooms we wished to see, which were truly worthy of the occasion. We then found that we had received this civility from no less a man than the Count de Semonville, Grand Referendary of the Chamber of Peers.

Paris, 5th day, 10th mo 20. 1814

We went this morning to the Bibliothèque du Roi in the Rue Richelieu and saw this vast collection of about 350,000 volumes. Many persons, old and young, were sitting reading at Tables in the different rooms, the whole being, like almost every thing french, open to the public. The only impediment was a guard, to see that no improper people entered, & a written request, 'Essuyez vos pieds, S.V.P.'

The Palais Bourbon, where the Chamber of Deputies assemble, is superb, even more so than the House of Peers, & the committee rooms, antirooms &ca, are very superior to any thing of the kind in England. We saw several deputies in costume, who bowed to us, & amongst the rest the President Lainée, in a very rich costume, with a large white silk sash.

We next went to the Hospital des Invalides, an establishment which I suppose Europe cannot equal, take it in all its parts. Its most striking feature is the Church, with its large dome, or rather cluster of

Domes, filled with painting & gilding & reverber-
ating Echo of every sound. The outside of the great
dome & its lofty spire are also richly gilt, & forms a
brilliant & magnificent feature in the view of Paris.
We saw the dinner serving for the officers, in number
from 2 to 300, & all on dishes of solid silver. We next
went to a plain beyond the Champs Elysées, hoping to
see the Marshals & Princes of France returning from
a Sham Fight, but they did not end the Battle till too
late, but we saw the operation a small distance off and
a tremendous firing of cannon and musquetry was
kept up, and it gave a strong idea of a real Battle.

We ascended Montmartre, where we had a most
striking and delightful view of Paris (alias Babylon),
a city containing more resources for the man of the
world than any other place under Heaven. I cannot
help liking Paris. I am getting to feel very much at
home here. One thing I have no doubt has more
effect than I am aware of, which is, that the air &
diet, & even water (filtered) unquestionably agree
with me better than those of England, & I awake in
a morning more refreshed, & freer from headaches.
NB. I think I have once or twice felt a flea, in the day
time, since I came to Paris, a week tomorrow—but

except that, I have neither seen or felt any species of Vermin.

Paris, 6th day. 10th mo 21. 1814
We set off in pretty good time, with Charles Buxton's party, for Versailles. In our way we took St Cloud; the exterior has nothing striking but the approach & fine garden in the old fashioned style. Some of the rooms are beautiful & fitted up with great taste & magnificence. The picture gallery contains some exquisite productions & some fine large vases of the Sevre porcelain. One or two of them are most beautiful likenesses of Bonaparte, in character, represented as holding Victory in subjection. This place is well worth visiting.

We next saw the famous porcelain manufactory of the Sevre, which we saw in great perfection, as in consequence of the Duchess of Angoulême being expected that morning, the finest specimens were arranged in great order for her inspection. We saw many articles of extraordinary beauty, and not less extraordinary *price*.

Versailles is now undergoing a thorough repair. 2,000 workmen were said to be employed in the palace when we were there, and in consequence of this, and of the absence of the Governor, we were unable to see the interior of this most stately pile. I should think the Palace of Versailles & its offices covered not much less than 40 acres of ground. It is of a regular form, & in a grand & fine stile of architecture. The prodigious gardens, walks and alleys & canals [are] decorated with profusion of statues of great beauty, with every fanciful variety of fountains & jets d'eau, formed at immense expence & which we were assured cannot now be all made to play, for about 2 to 3 hours, without an expence of 10,000 francs each time.

Its Orangeries containing 1200 trees, & its subordinate palaces of the Trianons, make Versailles an abode fit for the greatest monarch upon Earth, & as superior to any English palace, as the best of our palaces are to a parish workhouse!!

I was much pleased with the greater Trianon and the gardens of the Little Trianon, which are very pretty, & in the English taste. We returned fatigued, but much gratified with our excursion.

Paris, 7th day, 10th mo 22. 1814

We went this morning to the Parthenon, formerly the Church of Ste Genevieve, now appropriated as a burying place for senators, ex-officers & all illustrious persons. The inscription on the Pediment 'Aux grands homes, la Patrie reconnaissante' is strikingly appropriate. It contains in the vaults, which are dry & light, a vast number of small Chambers, each capable of containing 8 or 10 tombs, but few of which are began to be made use of. This is the Westminster Abbey of France, but as inferior to ours, as their palaces are superior to ours, and the same may be said in an equal degree in comparing the Cathedral of Notre Dame with our St Paul's.

We next proceeded to the Catacombs, & after waiting some little time were admitted with several others. After taking several wax tapers lighted, and a few unlighted in case of need, we entered through a small house, the staircase which leads down to these silent depositaries of the dead. We first descended with our guide a spiral stone staircase about 75 feet down, and proceeding along a great length of passage cut in the solid stone, with so many bye ways as to make us feel the utility of a guide, we came at length to a large handsome doorway, with a frame cut in the stone; over it an inscription, 'L'Empire des Morts', & urging a conduct suitable to the awful spectacle! We then entered, and after passing through a great length of way, returned by the same road.

The Catacombs consist of a series of passages cut in the stone, of unequal breadth, sometimes forming a considerable open space, with a rough column or two to support it, & having at suitable distances on blocks of stone in imitation of Altars and Tombstones inscriptions appropriate to the place. On such side the bones of countless myriads, but called 2,400.000 persons, lie arranged in order, the larger bones of thighs, arms &ca, outward, & in rows of close lines, one line about 2 feet above another, are placed the skulls, presenting a picture that speaks to the heart, & to which the imagination cannot be an indifferent spectator.

It is calculated to contain the remains of four times the number of the living inhabitants of Paris. I could not but feel impressed, but I should have been sorry not to have seen this place, from which we set off to finish our survey of the Jardin des Plantes, of which I have spoken elsewhere.

We next drove to the Champs de Mars, which is a large square enclosure, fit for Reviews or Public assemblies, with the ground raised sloping (round) at the edges, so as to allow vast numbers to stand a little elevated, and to see distinctly what passes in the space within. It stands behind the Ecole Militaire, a superb establishment, built in a fine & massy stile of architecture, and containing 4000 boys to be educated for the army.

Paris, 1st day, 10th mo 23. 1814

I went this morning to indulge in a warm bath & was tempted to try one at the Bains Virgier, which are two large establishments, like large Noah's Arks on the Seine. The accommodations were good, & except the floor, perfectly clean & comfortable. They brought me a hand-basin full of highly perfumed soap froth, which was very pleasant to use, but dear, as I paid 30 sous for it.

We dined at Frederick Faber's, the Banker, at Auteuil, about a league from Paris. We were very handsomely and kindly entertained. I was pleased with F's wife, & his wife's sister, also the eldest daughter, but most of all with the youngest daughter Camille, a very pretty and sweet girl. His eldest son, Edward, who is 27 years old, is the smallest man I ever saw; I should think not above 3 feet 9 inches high, but quite well formed, clever & intelligent.

The french customs altogether pleased me, except the mistress of the house, standing half way down the table to help the soup, & allowing no help in carving. The conversation was spirited and agreeable, & the ladies playful & unaffected. They would have liked music & billiards, but we made no scruple of a pointed objection to everything of the kind on that day of the week. By We, I mean to include the Buxtons, & particularly Amelia Henning, whose uniform consistancy of conduct & steadiness in what she apprehended right, was highly creditable to her. The ride was very pleasant, being all the way on the Banks of the Seine, very near which Auteuil is situated.

Paris, 2nd day, 10th mo 24. 1814
We were busy making our remaining purchases & preparing for our departure. On the 25th, we heard that David & Agatha Barclay had arrived at the 'Grange Bateliere' in the Rue Pinon, where I soon went. It was

remarkably pleasant meeting them & in the evening I went & met them at the Charles Buxtons at the Hotel d'Autriche. On the 26th, they & Barnard Hanbury came & breakfasted with us, & at ½ past 12 o'clock we set off & left Paris, not without a feeling of regret on all our parts, and on mine a hope, that a long time may not elapse before I see it again.

We slept at the Lion d'Or at Beauvais & had very comfortable quarters. The next day we travelled hard through a charming country, & reached Montreuil-sur-mer, a fortress on a small hill, where we had excellent accomodation.

At Airaines, not having time to alight for refreshment, I procured a bottle of wine which we drank off, & I got some excellent slices from a gigot de mouton roti, dressed as in England, & put it on a plate with some salt & slices of bread, & paying the charge, & placing it on our knees in the carriage, drove off in excellent humour.

I enquired at Nouvion the price of oats, and was informed they could buy the quarter of 8 bushels for 6 francs. At Nampont, I had a dispute with the maître de poste, an imposing scoundrel, & I told him so.

From Montreuil we reached Calais in the evening, by Boulogne,[1] a delightful situation, & the whole country we came through to it is extremely beautiful & interesting, & for a considerable way towards Calais, where we slept at Quillacque's. I thought them this time deficient in attention in the waiting department, & perhaps of the many places I have seen in France, Calais is one of those I like the least.

When we sailed the next morning, I observed my ladies & Martha B. looking plumper than in going out. Whether from causes above the skin, or under it, I leave to them to explain, but whatever it was, it was not a durable appearance, as I thought them much thiner a day or two after.[2]

We sailed at 11, & did not land till dusk. We had a fair wind, but too little of it, & most of us were dreadfully sick, viz C. & M. Buxton, Caroline, Eliza, Rachel, & myself, Amelia rather so, & only Katharine who escaped entirely. We could not make

[1] KF: *Our father omits to mention that at Boulogne we saw rotting in the harbour, or rather on the mud Banks, Buonaparte's famous fleet of flat bottomed boats, intended for the invasion of England.*

[2] KF: *The restrictions on french manufactures caused travellers to load themselves with extra clothing to enable them to bring home silk dresses, &ca.*

the harbour & had to encounter the rascality of the Dover Hovellers, who made us pay 5/ apiece to convey us a few score yards to the shore, where we were heartily glad to arrive & were most hospitably received & lodged at Thomas Beiks, receiving the kindest attention from him & his wife & son—and the next day set off for Plashet.

End of Joseph Fry's journal
October 1814

Katharine Fry grew up against the backdrop of war with France and her first trip across the Channel, at the age of thirteen, was in the autumn before the Battle of Waterloo. By the time she visited Normandy with her brother and sister thirteen years later, there had been peace for well over a decade. In England, the Regency was over and George IV was on the throne. There was a French king again, too, although the relatively liberal Louis XVIII had been succeeded by the decidedly illiberal Charles X.

Katharine was born in August 1801 at St Mildred's Court, London, the first of Elizabeth and Joseph Fry's eleven children. Two brothers and two sisters followed in the next seven years, including William and Richenda, her companions in Normandy. In 1809, the family left London and moved to their estate at Plashet. Four more children arrived before the even tenor of their life in the country was broken up by a financial crisis in 1816. A temporary return to London and a shortage of money and space meant that the elder children were despatched to live with their mother's relatives. Katharine and Rachel, the two eldest, went to their uncle Daniel Gurney and his unmarried sister at Runcton, near King's Lynn. Daniel was only ten years older than Katharine and they became great friends. Many years later, in 1845, after she had been helping him with his *Record of the House of Gurney*, he wrote to her:

> *I must send you one line to say how sorry I am to part with you and how very much I have enjoyed your company. As we wend on in life one of the most delightful things that can befall us is to find that those who have years back suited us, and our tastes and habits, go on doing so, and the renewal of these is a rare pleasure.*

Staying at Runcton allowed Katharine and Rachel to experience life away from the stricter Quaker regulations operating at the time. Though Elizabeth Fry's faith had grown ever stronger, her young brother's ties with the Society had slackened and he later left it altogether. Elizabeth was worried about the influence of 'those not Friends' on her girls but Katharine was convinced that their more relaxed education in Norfolk helped them to cope with the demands which would soon be made on them:

> *Had we entered ... on the life our Mother's engagement opened for us fresh from the seclusion of our schoolroom at Plashet, and the restraints and prejudices of the strict and exclusive Quakerism to which we had been trained, we should have been unfit for it, and comparatively useless. During the year spent in Norfolk, we had passed out of childhood into womanhood. Young and inexperienced indeed we were but we had seen a little of general society, and become accustomed to its usages...*

Elizabeth Fry, more and more involved in her prison work and increasingly respected and consulted by the authorities, was starting to realise how much she would need her daughters' help. In 1817 she wrote to them: 'You must, my loved girls, industriously do your part ... we must none of us be idle and as you are now come to an age of some understanding, I hope to find you real helpers.'

They were. Back at St Mildred's Court that winter, aged sixteen and fourteen, they worked on the enormous quantity of correspondence that Elizabeth received every day.

Our lives at St Mildred's Court were at this time indescribably full. Our drawing room far more resembled an office than a drawing room in a private house. The letters from all parts of the country to enquire the particulars of her plan were almost innumerable. Ladies wished to form committees to visit female prisoners, magistrates to improve their condition ... Besides these were petitions from prisoners everywhere... Poor people, and afflicted people, thinking her means as boundless as her good will, wrote countless petitions ... Also the personal and written application from persons, often of consequence, to request her to name a day for being allowed to visit Newgate with her ... The whole of this press of business was got through with no other assistance than Rachel and I were able to afford her.

It was an exciting, stimulating time. Elizabeth's public work was bringing her daughters into direct contact with the great and the good, and people of fashion and note. Some relatives felt that the two girls were getting above themselves. Their aunt Rachel Gurney wrote to reprove Joseph for his obvious pride in his daughters' abilities:

The sentiments of Vanity in a Parent's mind are quickly enough discerned by the child... [Your girls] perceive that your vanity is excited by their quickness and by such acquirements as they have; and to this there is a quick responsive chord in their minds, that is far too much alive! And there is a high spirit in both of them, about themselves, their talents, their situation &ca that I have most truly labored ... to show them the folly of, and the absolute necessity of its being brought under subjection to the Christian principle and spirit.

Maria Edgeworth, too, visiting the family about this time, dismissed Katharine as 'too pert and talkative'. Such impressions are a contrast to the picture given of Katharine later in life by the travel diaries and Family Record, where she appears rather an anxious pilgrim, very aware of her responsibilities.

It seemed that whatever the girls did, they were bound to be criticised by one side or the other. They were being trained to do valuable work at a time when many of their contemporaries were offered nothing more taxing than a piece of embroidery, but they were not to take any pride in their achievement. They were mixing in fashionable society, but they still had to wear the subdued Quaker dress. Their mother, supported by her faith, rejoiced in the costume (though it had to be of the finest materials) but her daughters felt conspicuous and feared they were being laughed at. Looking back, Katharine reflected on the impossible position they were in and the problems caused by

> the singular variety of influences to which we were exposed, and the singular variety of circumstances in which we were placed. In some circles we were looked upon as the simplest, plainest dressed young Quakers, in others as almost sinfully worldly and fashionable, and a reproach to our mother. [I was] not allowed to choose the shape of my own bonnet, or discression as to the use of the singular or plural pronoun in conversation.

Katharine's rebellion was not against the fundamentals of Quakerism, however—only its outward forms, 'the quaintness and formality of their manners … their peculiarities of address and behaviour'. Years later, in a letter to her mother in 1827, she tried to explain what she felt:

> As much as I am anything I am a Friend in the root, and believe I shall never even wish to join

any other body, but I am so penetrated with the
opinion that the work of religion is a spiritual
work only, that it lies alone between Man and
his Maker, and if we carefully follow, according
to our ability, the pointings of duty in our own
hearts, it is enough: and I hardly know how to
endure hearing stress laid on little matters by one
man for another… I cannot bring myself to care
what people are called, or according to what form
they worship, what they feel themselves at liberty
to do, or what to leave undone…

Meanwhile, there was much to enjoy. In 1820
Joseph and Elizabeth took Katharine and Rachel
on a tour of England, which combined sightseeing
and socialising with prison visits and business meetings. Katharine remembered a visit to the Danbys at
Swinton, ten miles from Ripon, where their sketches
were much admired by 'a large party of ladies and
gentlemen'. So too, apparently, was seventeen year-
old Rachel. The Frys had left Swinton and were staying at an inn in Market Leighton, when

a post chaise rattled in, which after discussions
heard in the street, and about half an hour's
pause, rattled out again. Our father suppressed

till the morning the information that it contained
one of our Swinton friends, who was following us,
and made to our father in the damp, dark night a
formal proposal of marriage for our sister Rachel,
which our father then and there refused on score
of Quakerism.

Rachel, it seems, had no say in the matter. Seven years later in France, her sister Richenda proved similarly alluring but there is no record of Katharine's hand being sought by anyone. She was the only one of her brothers and sisters to stay single. Rachel was the first to marry. Because her husband (like the Swinton suitor) was not a Friend, and Quaker rules at the time meant that parents could not be seen to condone a marriage 'out' by attending the ceremony, Joseph and Elizabeth were not present. Nor were Katharine and Richenda, who consoled themselves by watching— and in Katharine's case, drawing—King George IV's coronation procession.

Life at Plashet in the 1820s was astonishingly full and entertaining, with a never-ending influx of family and friends, dignitaries, philanthropists, and foreigners with letters of introduction to Mrs Fry. These included distinguished Italian refugees, a party of

Canadian Indians who 'came over to treat with the English Government respecting some grievance' and two Mexicans, 'singularly elegant and pleasing young men,' who entertained the party by demonstrating how to lasso the Plashet cows. There was even the odd visit from royalty. By now Katharine had taken over responsibility for running the house and it was she who had to deal with an unexpected visit from the Crown Princess of Denmark. She remembered the panic it caused the household:

Alas, for the housekeeper, dear old Atherton, for Crawley the cook, and for the deputy mistress, the unfortunate eldest daughter, who had to arrange at an hour's notice for a royal guest at the mid-day meal… and a large dinner party at night.

She coped with aplomb, however, offering royalty 'the good fare prepared for the dinner', and ordering a hamper from town 'whose contents furnished forth the otherwise dilapidated dinner.'

For their summer holidays, the family escaped to two cottages, which 'resembled a primitive highland inn', on the banks of Dagenham Breach. In the solitude of the marshes and accessible only by water, it was an ideal place for relaxing and messing about in

71

boats. For the rest of the year, Elizabeth was often away on long, demanding tours. In early 1827, she spent three months in Ireland with her brother and, while her mother and uncle inspected prisons and lunatic asylums and attended Meetings of Friends, Katharine held the reins at Plashet.

Her turn for a trip came later that year, when she, William and Richenda set off on their own in August:

> *Our brother William, Chenda and myself started for a month's trip in Normandy. The old green travelling carriage, that performed the Irish journey with our mother, was put in requisition and, attended by a courier, we left Plashet on the 1st of August and arrived at Le Havre after a stormy passage from Southampton on the 4th.*

Like her father in 1814, Katharine kept a diary of the tour, with contributions from her brother and sister; like her father, she was an eager traveller, recording coaches and inns, castles and cathedrals with lively interest. But there the resemblance between the diaries ends. Joseph gives the high-spirited impression of travel for travel's sake: the sheer enjoyment of discovering another country. Katharine's journal is,

*Joseph Fry, c 1820
painted by Charles Robert Leslie*

Elizabeth Fry, 1818
Engraving by J. Thomson,
based on a miniature painting by Samuel Drummond

Plashet House
as it appeared in 1808; from a
sketch by Richenda Gurney

Above: Plashet House in 1808, by Richenda Gurney
Below: Runcton in 1815, by Daniel Gurney

Above: Cottages at Dagenham, where the Frys spent summer holidays
Below: Coronation of George IV (both sketches by Katharine Fry)

The Fry children in 1830
drawing by Charlotte Giberne

'And this seems the proper place to introduce a photograph, taken from a drawing of the group of seven brothers and sisters who accompanied our parents from Plashet and settled at Upton Lane in 1829. It was drawn by Miss Charlotte Gibbern, about the year 1830, whilst the party still retained the dress of Friends. William and Joseph stand at the back of the group. Of William it conveys a tollerable idea and is the only likeness of him that we know of. Hannah and Louisa are seated, both dressed in white, Louisa has little Rattle in her arms. Katharine in black satin forms the centre of the group, and Harry, a child, stands at her knee. Gurney, quite a boy, holds a book in his hand.' (Family Record)

Above: left, William Storrs Fry, 1832; right, flowers by Katharine Fry
Below: the Frys' house at Upton Lane

Richenda Reynolds and her daughters,
Richenda Elizabeth and Esther Marianne, in 1873.

Joseph Fry at 81

'His personal courage was great: nothing seemed to frighten him. He was rather under the middle size, stout, but a very good figure and beautifully formed limbs. In conclusion, we may say of him that though he did not emulate our mother in her great deeds and works of Charity, he never opposed her, and always held up her hands, taking great care of her bodily, as well as often encouraging her mentally.' (Family Record) for a variety of reasons, more subdued and complex. Because she had been well trained by her mother, their itinerary in Normandy had to include a more serious objective than mere sightseeing: they were also to tour prisons, schools and hospitals, making careful notes of their findings. There is, too, an undercurrent of complicated human relationships in the diary, which rarely breaks surface but nevertheless creates a tension. And there is the shadow cast by Richenda's illness.

The first part of the journal is, however, serene, despite the horrors of a night in Portsmouth harbour and a rough crossing. Katharine gives as lively an account of early 19th-century travel as her father could have done.

> ... *no one, who has not experienced what it is to pass a night on a hard mattress laid on a locker; and ride out a gale of wind in a harbour, can imagine the uncomfortableness of it. The noise of the water, the whistling of the wind in the cordage, the rocking of the ship, aided by swarms of fleas, almost banished sleep.*

And, once across the Channel, she finds travelling by post an entertaining experience:

> *We are posting with three horses abreast, the oddest*
> *looking creatures ever beheld. The harness patched*
> *up of rope & leather, the saddles high before and*
> *behind like those we see in ancient pictures. The*
> *postilions as odd as their horses.*

Sometimes, too, a gleam of her father's dry humour
shows through. She is very taken with William the
Conqueror's castle at Falaise and does several draw-
ings, but is sceptical about the guide's anecdotes:

> *From one of these windows, which our guide*
> *pointed out to us, Duke Robert is said to have seen*
> *the famous Arletta washing clothes in the reservoir*
> *below, where we saw many women still occupied*
> *in the same manner, but we thought it impossible*
> *that Duke Robert could have distinguished her*
> *beauty, unless his sight was wonderfully long.*

William, in the manner of Joseph in Paris, strolls
out in the evening to mix with the locals. He is struck
by their sobriety, compared to the English: 'The horse
dealers and people of that class were drinking nothing
but Café or Eau-Sucré.' All three Frys are fascinated
by the Bayeux tapestry, 'kept with a good deal of care,
on a large roller, though such frequent winding and
unwinding must be injurious to such old materials'.

Only Richenda is less than inspired by some of the places they visit: 'We were ferried over to see a church neither ancient, nor beautiful, where a poor idiot was walking up and down.'

A more serious, conscientious tone creeps in when the Frys begin their fact-finding missions. These are undertaken in the company of their Caen friends, including two young French doctors, Pelletier and Martin. William approves of the hospital and the 'very pretty, nice looking, rather young' Abbess at the orphanage, but it is left to Katharine to describe the more sombre visits to the central prison and the town gaol, to detail the accommodation, food, clothing and activities, and to conclude that there was 'an intention to do well by the prisoners, but a total ignorance of the simplist principles of Prison Discipline'. Saddest of all were the condemned cells 'in which they are kept sometimes as long as six weeks ... light and air only admitted through a grated hole communicating with a dismal passage'.

Threads of concern about Richenda, almost invisible at first, run through the diary. She is very seasick on the crossing out and is carried down to the cabin by the captain who 'nursed her with the skill and tenderness of a woman'. With the stewardess also ill, Katharine is grateful to the captain, who 'was continually in our cabin; had it not been for him I know not what would have become of poor Chenda, she was continually fainting.' His kindness and attention to the young Frys when the crossing was over, showing them round Le Havre, escorting them on a drive to Orchet and seeing them on to their boat to Honfleur, are mentioned appreciatively.

What is omitted—but made clear in the Family Record nearly half a century later—is that the captain had an ulterior motive: he had fallen in love with Richenda. At the end of their time in Normandy, he wrote to tell Katharine of his passion for her sister. William had already returned to England but the young French doctor, Pelletier, sent him a letter:

Il est nécessaire que vous sachez que votre Capitaine Brais [Brice] a eu la folie de concevoir pour Mlle Richenda un interêt tellement vif, qu'on pourrait je crois sans se tromper l'appeler Amour.

The captain was given no encouragement: Katharine and their Caen circle decided that the best course of action was to appear not to understand him.

Richenda's minor indispositions early in the tour

assume alarming proportions when the Frys are about to leave Caen and she is taken violently ill. The hastily summoned Irish doctor diagnoses inflammation of the bowels, bleeds her 'copiously', and prescribes 'the most violent medecines'. For three days she lies ill, 'raving in a sort of hysterical dilirium' while the doctor continues the same extreme treatment. The diary is full of Katharine's feeling of helplessness and foreboding:

> *I thought of home; of our parents; of the strength of*
> *a many times twisted cord at such moments: and*
> *then the sensation of my lonely desolate situation*
> *came over me like an oppressive cloud.*

Two things emerge clearly from her account of the illness. One, of course, is the frighteningly crude, haphazard nature of medicine at the time; the other is Richenda's highly emotional state. She is in such a pitch of 'weakness and nervous irritation' that she cannot bear to see Katharine. The diary logs the tense days until Katharine summons up courage to dismiss the Irish doctor and call in a French physician. Recovery is rapid and they can enjoy life again:

> *Our evenings ... become brighter and brighter as*
> *they are more near ceasing for ever. All our friends*

regularly spend them with us. Coffee and syrops
are our refreshment whilst singing, and Monsieur
Pelletier's guitar, together with poetry, conversa-
tion, and that inexpressible charm that accompa-
nies the unrestrained intercourse of friends.

Despite her improved health, Richenda is still in
a mercurial state. As the sisters make their farewells,
Richenda becomes 'overcome and hysterical' at taking
leave of their friends, the Sherwells, and Katharine is
'forced to go home alone to the Hotel for dinner and
send a carriage up for her'. Meanwhile M. Martin,
one of the young French doctors, surprises them
'by his appearance ... whilst we were at Coffee' and
spends a last day with them.

It is clear that more has occurred in Caen than has
been committed to the diary. Katharine, so anxious
to fill the gaps in her father's journal, is more circum-
spect in her own. Her account of finally leaving the
town with Richenda is a masterpiece of the unsaid:

We drove silent, and thoughtful out of Caen, a
place frought with most interesting recollections
for us, and one which I shall never forget.

Tour in Normandy, 1827

by Katharine, Richenda and William Storrs Fry

We left Plashet August the first, 1827, to make a tour in Normandy. The party consisted of William, Katharine and Richenda. We were attended by only one travelling servant, a frenchman; we also took an English travelling carriage.

We arrived at Southampton the same evening and found to our great disappointment that the packet for Havre-de-Grace did not sail till Friday evening. Making, however, the best of our misfortune, we spent the next day, Thursday, in going in the same packet, in which we were to cross to Havre, to see the Regatta off the Isle of Wight.

The scene was remarkably animated: multitudes of the prettiest little yatchts, belonging to the Yatcht Club, as well as all the pleasure boats the neighbouring ports could produce. Cowes and Ryde looked well from the water, and appearantly full of Company. At the former place we landed for half an hour and met to our surprise and pleasure our Mexican friends, Gambetta and the two Gutierreys, who are waiting at Portsmouth for the Frigate to convey them to Mexico.

Friday morning at length arrived, and with it a good deal of wind—so much as to prevent our going to see Netley Abbey. The afternoon was not more favourable, and when we embarked on board the 'St David', it was 'blowing very fresh' and contrary for our passage. As we got out of the Southampton River, the weather became worse and the Captain thought proper to put into Portsmouth Harbour for the night. William went on shore in search of our Mexican friends, who in about an hour returned with him, and we passed a happy, merry evening on the poop deck, supping in darkness and not knowing till we tasted it, what we were eating.

The scene around us was highly interesting. The busy sailors in the Port with their boats, the fine men of war at anchor, the Town, the Magazines, &ca. As the evening closed in, the men of war fired a Royal Salute in honor of the Duke of Clarence (afterwards King William IV) who was in the town, firing round by turns, and the echo from side to side added to the effect. The noise was too much to be agreeable, the flashes from the guns looked like lightening. Then the lights from the town and the different ships were extremely pretty.

About 10 o'clock we went to bed, but no one, who has not experienced what it is to pass a night on a hard mattress laid on a locker and ride out a gale of wind in a harbour, can imagine the uncomfortableness of it. The noise of the water, the whistling of the wind in the cordage, the rocking of the ship, aided by swarms of fleas, almost banished sleep, and we gladly obeyed William's summons at ½ past 3 to get up and see the vessel weigh and get out. The wind still blew, but every one hoped it would go down as the day advanced, and the St David is so fine a vessel, built on purpose for rough winter seas between Liverpool & Dublin, & the crew so efficient, that even should the weather not improve, there was no cause for uneasiness. When, however, we had passed the Isle of Wight, into the open sea, we found that we had no trifle to encounter. The breeze had become a regular gale and, to use the Captain's words, there was a *very heavy sea on*.

By 8 o'clock, the passengers, 50 in number, were nearly all ill. The vessel piched and rolled, the wind set onto the starboard bow, and seas were breaking over the deck every moment. Chenda fainted. We made her up a bed under the shelter of a hatch-way with the cusheons of our carriage. William was already ill. Chenda became too ill to remain on deck; the Captain carried her into the cabin, laid her in a berth, and attended to her with the greatest kind-ness. Kneeling over her and following her into the cabin soon made me sufficiently poorly to be glad to lay down, and to be incapable of helping her. There were very few ladies on board and they were all *ill* but myself, and I was only poorly.

The sea was a grand, but awful sight out of the stern Cabin window, bright green, the waves the hight of hills, each crested every moment by the wind, with green feathers tipped with white. Our ship rode over them beautifully. At the time I compared her to a Sea Bird swimming among the breakers. Add to this, every thing was so quiet, no loud bauling or calling out. The Captain was continually in our cabin; had it not been for him I know not what would have become of poor Chenda, she was continually faint-ing. The stewardess was ill herself, and he nursed her with the skill and tenderness of a woman.

The weather moderated about 4 o'clock in the

afternoon. I soon went on deck. About five, we were able to go up onto the poop deck and Chenda was carried up there, where she lay very faint, till the sight of Havre put every one into spirits. A little after seven o'clock we got into the harbour, and enjoyed the luxury of being able to stand and walk. Then succeeded the bustle of landing: 'Les duaniers' came on board, luggage carrying to the Custom House, &ca, &ca. At length we gladly established ourselves at the 'Hotel de Londres' kept by English people and on the whole very comfortable. Bed was our chief desire, where we retired early.

Havre, Sunday August 5th, 1827
This morning we were awoke early by the constant chattering of the people at a fountain under our windows; there were assembled about twenty men, women and children, waiting for their turns to fill a couple of little pails that they carry on a large hoop. The costumes pretty and very different from ours in England, but we have observed very few of the high Norman caps.

After breakfast we walked about the town conducted by our kind Captain of the St David. We went

into the principal Church, where was a large congregation of well dressed people, chiefly women, without
hats, or bonnets but wearing every variety of caps, &
hearing mass. Several of them wore the high Norman
cap. We then walked through the streets. The place
has the appearance of much commerce: three basins
filled with ships from all parts of the world, multitudes of parots at the houses, the large douanne and
the number of sailors bespeak it. The Captain told us
that Havre is now considered the principal port of
France for trade with America, the Brazils, and the
East and West Indies. We passed through the fruit
market, which was abundantly supplied, and walked
outside the fortifications. The country beyond appears
to be beautiful, the hights round the town are well
wooded, and the many houses built of white stone
add much to the landscape.

Returning to our Hotel, we passed a few quiet
hours in reading and writing till five o'clock, the
hour of the Table d'hôte, where we dined with several
of our fellow passengers of the St David, the dinner
quite in the English fashion. After it, we walked into
the suberbs, where it seemed as if all Havre was turned
out: the people very well dressed, most of the women

without bonnets, the colouring brilliant, the walks lined with groups of people sitting and chatting, the shops all open. In one place were rope dancers, in another there was a man inviting the company, with stentorian lungs, to come and witness a comedy.

We have made up a party to go tomorrow to Orchet, a beautiful spot on the Siene about three leagues off.

Monday August 6th, 1827
This morning a party from the hotel set off after breakfast, conducted by Captain Brice of the St David, and went to see some Osage Indians just landed: four men & two women, fine handsome creatures, on the whole better looking than our old friends the Canadians. They are going to Paris and thence to London. At ten o'clock a Calêche, drawn by two small Norman horses, arrived to convey us to Orchet. The party consisted besides ourselves of Captain Brice, who William thought proper to ask, as a little mark of attention for his extreme kindness on board the packet, and one of our fellow travellers, who we call 'The Doctor' as he has told us that he is a medical man. He has travelled all over Europe, speaks

all the languages, and seems a thoroughly sensible, intelligent person.

We drove first onto the higths, called Coté St Michael, a lovely spot with many agreeable country residences: the views of the Town, Port, mouth of the Seine and the sea delightful. Thence to Harfleur. Of this little town we say nothing, as it is better told in Dawson Turner's book. The church is conspicuous for the beauty of its spire. We proceeded to Montravilliers, and afterwards to Orchet, the former a clean little country town with a stream running through it, in which many women were washing clothes.

Richenda takes the pen. We stopped at a lovely little auberge at Orchet. It was the fête des bouchers, several nice looking girls, prettily dressed, and gallant looking youths were about to begin dancing quadrilles, and a middle aged man was tuning his violin, leaning against a large apple tree, which shaded the whole group. After we were refreshed with vin-du-pays and bread and butter, we set off with a pretty little girl for our guide to see the Chateau, which in itself is in no way striking but the views from the terrace were magnificent. The cliffs were awfully steep, the tops covered with verdure, & the lower parts entirely white chalk, a beautiful contrast to the rich and varied colors of the Seine, upon which scarcely a ripple was to be seen. On our right hand in the distance stood Havre and oposite on the left, the pretty town of Honfleur, but in short it was a scene that no pen can describe. As a tout ensemble we are perfectly charmed with the views on the banks of this lovely river. We returned home just in time for the Table d'hôte, after which we walked on the pier with some of our English friends. It was a lovely evening, the sky almost cloudless, and the full moon, just risen, shed a silver light upon the winding Seine. After caffé we took our usual seat on the benches outside our hotel. William walked with Monsieur le docteur and then we went to bed, being as usual quite ready for it.

Tuesday August 7th, 1827
Katharine here resumes the pen. This morning we rose and packed up ready to start for Honfleur. Our friends of the St David accompanied us on board the Honfleur boat and about seven o'clock we left the harbour of Havre. A most agreeable, cheerful, busy place, devoid, however, of any objects of antiquarian interest. We were about an hour & a half crossing

the mouth of the Seine to Honfleur, the steward performing at intervals on a drum and Panpipes. The hights about Honfleur look extremely well from the water. The Town itself is situated in a valley, or what would in Somersetshire be called a 'Combe', of which country I am constantly reminded in the general effect of the landscape, on the banks of the Seine, and at its mouth. There is, however, one feature in which they differ, viz. the great number of Lombardy Poplars that are here to be seen, producing a very pleasing effect.

One of our fellow passengers of the St David, 'the Doctor', was also our companion de voyage in the present instance. We all breakfasted together at the Hotel d'Angleterre, newly established and kept by an Englishman, which they assured us was kept up in the English style; but an upper room with a brick floor, the walls hung with greasy painted tapestry, a few chairs, and a long deal table in the middle, did not recall English luxury to our minds. The breakfast that was shortly after spread on the aforesaid table still less resembled it, but we were hungry and merry, and soon left it to ascend the hights on the side of the town towards the sea, called the Côte de Grace.

Havre-de-Grace, from the Côte-de-Grace
near the Chapel de Notre Dame de Grace, KF 1827

It is a very high hill, the top covered with the most delightful trees and commanding extensive views of the Seine, of the Sea, &ca.

The foreground resembled Greenwich Park on a bold scale. The distant views were finer. A chapel is there, appearantly of great repute among sailors, called 'Notre Dame de Grace'. It was hung round with pictures of ships at sea in great difficulties, in which was always to be seen in the clouds a Virgin & Child coming to the rescue. These pictures were vowed by the Captains and crews at the moment of their danger.

From Honfleur, the road to Caen passes for the first stage through country of a similar character to that round le Havre; afterwards, though always in a state of high cultivation, it became less interesting. Fruit trees abound, and give even to the corn fields the appearance of orchards. The dresses of the peasantry increasingly picturesque: the high caps almost universal, except where a man's nightcap is substituted for it, in which tasteless article of dress the little babies even are sometimes to be seen.

We are posting *with three horses abreast*, the oddest looking creatures ever beheld. The harness patched up of rope & leather, the saddles high before and behind like those we see in ancient pictures. The postilions as odd as their horses. In harnessing them to the carriage they do not regard putting them at uneven distances from it; the one the postilion rides is always forward enough to prevent his leg from touching the shaft. When setting off, he shouts and cracks his whip vigourously, and continues to do so all the journey. It is the most noisy operation that can be imagined but somehow or other the horses contrive to scramble over the ground at the rate of six or seven miles an hour.

We arrived at Caen about seven o'clock in the evening, at the Hotel de la Place Royal, where we are comfortably accomodated.

Caen, Wednesday August 8th, 1827
After breakfast, we started to perambulate the town, accompanied by our old fellow traveller, 'the Doctor'. After first lounging into a bookseller's shop, we went to the Church of St Jean. It is so much blocked up with houses that it is almost impossible to see it. The building is in the Pointed style.

Our equipage in Normandy with our English travelling carriage,
from nature, drawn by Wm S. Fry in 1827

W. S. Fry scripsit. We next went to the Cathedral dedicated to 'St Piere', which is much to be admired for the richness and beauty of the architecture, the Church of Notre Dame and the 'Abbaye aux hommes', in which we saw the tomb of William the Conqueror—for further particulars of these interesting churches see Turner's Normandy.

Richenda scrip. We dined at the Table d'hôte, with a large party of frenchmen, and one or two chatty women, who made so great a noise that we could scarsely understand one another speak. After dinner we took a long walk with our usual companion in the Prairie, where the soldiers were exercising, and after resting on the banks of the little river Orne, we were ferried over to see a church neither ancient, nor beautiful, where a poor idiot was walking up and down. When the evening closed we went back to our hotel, to take Café, our favourite répas. The Doctor (a fellow traveller in the steamer) took leave of us and after drawing and writing for about an hour, we went to bed.

The next morning, the 9th, we rose early, and after breakfast Katharine went to sketch some of the Churches, and at eleven o'clock we went to our kind

Caen Bridge over the River Orne from the Grand Course, KF 1827

friends the Abbotts, who took us to join a party to go over the beautifully arranged hospital, which was formerly a Royal Convent.

William scrip: Chenda has omitted to say that after seeing the Churches yesterday morning, we went over the Hotel de Ville, a handsome stone building occupying one side of the square of the Place Royale. The only things we saw to interest us were the town library and a gallery of paintings, none of which merit description. But to return to the 'Hopital des Dames', it is built on the site of the old Abbaye aux Dames, which was built & endowed by Matilda, wife

of William the Conqueror. Almost the only part of the abbey left standing is used by the present nuns for their devotions. Katharine was in raptures with the fine old architecture; some rare arches took her fancy greatly. I will try to explain by hieroglific what I cannot express in words, a sort of double arch in some of the windows, which she had not time to sketch. Underneath is a curious old crypt. We were shown down into it with candles. A few years ago were discovered here in a sarcophagus the bones of Cicily, daughter of William the Conqueror, & first abbess of this convent. There were also some bones found in the walls of this place, which tradition states to be the bones of some unhappy nuns bricked up alive for some sin.

It was a matter of favour seeing through the Hospital; we were conducted there by Mrs Sherwell, a friend of the Abbotts, who knew two of the medical gentlemen Mesieurs Peltier and Martin. These gentlemen were extremely polite; they showed us through the whole establishment, which took us three hours. Every thing seemed beautifully arranged, the rooms airy and clean, the beds not too close together; in fact, nothing seemed wanting to accelerate the cure of the patients. Baths of every description, food of every description, with the best medical attendance. The only nurses are thirty nuns, of the order of St Augustine, who never quit the walls, to whom the neatness & order may be in great measure attributed. The dress of these truly amiable women is white, with a black veil. We saw no religious books, and in some of the wards the men were playing at cards. In the hospitals I saw in Paris [they] had Bibles and other serious books, lent them by the priest. In all institutions of this sort, the French shine; I attribute it in great measure to the 'Soeurs de Charité'. My friend Monsieur Appert says 'Elles sont de veritables Anges!'

We returned to our hotel to dress, and afterwards to dine and spend the evening at Mr and Mrs Abbott's, where we met Mrs Sherwell and the two french Doctors. The time passed sociably away. We have made an engagement to return to Caen for two days next week, in order to see the great prison of the Department, the Hospital of St Louis, the Foundling Hospital and the lunatic asylum.

I am so tired I make nothing but mistakes, and

it being near midnight, I shall say goodnight, mes amis!

Friday August 10th, 1827

This morning we set off early for Falaise, where we arrived about one o'clock. Katharine and William went off to see the curiosities of the place; Chenda, being a good deal overdone, remained at our Inn, 'Le grand Turc', and one to which we can recommend our friends.

The drive from Caen to Falaise was through a flat, and uninteresting country but, like all of Normandy that we have seen, highly cultivated. Falaise is situated in a valley and takes its name from the rocks which are close to the town, and on which its noble old castle is built, one of the most beautiful and interesting remains of midieval splendour it was ever my lot to see. The 'Keep' or Donjon is built on a high, bold Rock overhanging the town. Except in the parts where the precipitous rocks rendered it unassailable, it was defended by a high wall, flanked at regular intervals by circular bastions, still perfect. The keep is square, with flat Norman buttresses, and the upper story windows are in very pure Norman style. The little pillars and their capitals, instead of the Capitals of a later date, are sculptured. From one of these windows, which our guide pointed out to us, Duke Robert is said to have seen the famous Arletta (or Hurletta) washing clothes in the reservoir below, where we saw many women still occupied in the same manner, but *we* thought it impossible that Duke Robert could have distinguished her beauty, unless his sight was wonderfully long.

Attached to the Norman keep was a square projection with pointed windows and the remains of transoms and mullions. This part a good deal resembled

Le chateau de Falaise de la route de Vire, KF 1827

the part of Castle Rising in Norfolk known as Queen Eleanor's apartments. But the most striking feature of the Castle of Falaise is a magnificent Tower, joined to the Keep by a bridge, and making, if I may so express myself, the Keep of the Keep. Tradition says it was built by Talbot, the English governor of the place, but it was in fact built by King Henry V of England. It is a hundred feet high, circular and of the most beautiful masonry. It appears to have originally contained seven stories; two apartments retain their vaulted roofs, the lowest of these has no apperture to admit the light, and may have been the dungeon, or a store house; the others are only lighted by small loopholes. Little staircases made in the solid wall lead from room to room and are in such good repair that we [were] able to go from the top to the bottom of the Tower without difficulty.

We returned to our Inn highly interested by what we had seen and, finding Chenda better, William and I went to explore the rocks facing the castle, which are craggy and bold, reminding us a little of the High Rocks at Tonbridge Wells, only these at Falaise are very superior. In mentioning the Tower I have omitted to mention that in the wall, which is twelve feet

The Keep of Falaise Castle from the interior of the courtyard, KF 1827

thick towards the top, and still thicker at the base, is a well communicating with all the stories. But to return to the Rocks, 'falaise', opposite, to which we ascended with considerable difficulty, from which the view was very fine.

In the evening we visited the Churches, which are old & florid, particularly that at Guibray, an adjoining village where a great fair is annually held, which has already commenced by a horse market. William says many of them were nice looking horses. The Norman horses appear to me not so well broke as ours in England, but gifted with more gentle natures, to supply the defects of art in their education.

In the evening William strolled out, and was struck by the sobriety that prevailed, compared to what a similar occasion would have induced in England. The horse dealers and people of that class were drinking nothing but Café or Eau-Sucré.

Saturday August 11th, 1827

We started in good time for Vire, a distance of twelve leagues. The first part of the journey was through a delightful country, hilly and reminding us of Somersetshire. From Condé to Vire we travelled through a district known as the 'Boccage' which, as its name implies, was very woody. The fields seperated by hedges, with abundance of hedge-row trees, brought the Western parts of England more & more to our minds.

We arrived at Vire by three o'clock, intending to remain there that night at least, but how can I describe the dirt, the filth of the Inn that prevented us from persuing this plan! Our country has not in it such a reality; the language therefore wants the power to express it: every thing was *black* with dirt, and the smell, no one who has not smelt it can conceive. They showed us a bed room. The bed furniture of silk had once been green, the walls were hung with ancient tapestry, the devices of which were effaced with dirt, the floor was far dirtier than a street, for that is sometimes washed by the rain but this for years can never have known the administration of mop or broom. We determined to go away and get to St Lo, a distance of nine leagues, after dinner. Whilst that was preparing, we walked about the town. The streets are extremely narrow & close, and the houses projecting in many of the streets over a sort of low arched footway where were the shops, at one of which we bought a pair of Sabots for Harry, appearantly the principal manufacture of the place.

But now to describe our dinner, which we took off a dirty cloth, spread at the end of a long deal table, in a room which perfectly harmonised with the rest of the piece and communicated with a kitchen that for blackness, smoke and horror rivals the cave of Leonora in Gil Blas. From this nasty receptible came first cabbage soup, half grease, then a boiled duck and a roast chicken, both high. In short, had not our courier Nicholas contrived to do us some good mutton chops and make a salad, we must have starved.

Thankfully did we escape to our carriage, and

driving out of the town of Vire breath once more the clear air of heaven.

The country between Vire and St Lo is some of the most beautiful we ever saw; in parts it was quite sublime. The bold hills with precipitous rocky sides, rapid rivers flowing through the ravines, valleys full of woods, the brows of the hills purple with heath in flower, made us doubly regret being obliged to hurry on to St Lo, without stopping to sketch; but evening was coming on, the roads were bad and the weather stormy.

We got to St Lo between eight and nine o'clock, and soon established ourselves in quarters that after Vire appeared tollerable, but are in fact dirty in the rooms but clean in the 'dentrées'. We intend to remain here over tomorrow, as we hear that the Inn at Bayeux is dirty. We begin to long for the luxuries of the Hotel Royal at Caen.

Sunday August 12th, 1827
We breakfast in the Salle à Manger. In french inns there are no private sitting rooms, but one large room for the eatings of all the guests: 'salle à manger'. We took our coffee, eggs, &ca, at one end of a long table,

at the other end of which three frenchmen were breakfasting off Cider, hot and cold meat, fruit &ca.

At ten o'clock we went to the Cathedral to hear 'La grande messe'. We sat on chairs in one of [the] ailes of the Chancel, where we had a full view of the Altar. The congregation was large and it was evidently a very solemn occasion: ten or twelve priests, besides boys, officiated. Five wore gaudy copes. Of the ceremony I shall say nothing but that it did not accord with our views of the spiritual worship of God. Neither the ministers, nor those to whom they ministered, looked very devout, except a few old women, and a widow by me. The countenances of the Priests had an expression of assumed solemnity that was far from agreeable and the sacredness of the office in which they were engaged did not prevent their looking at us with, I believe, as much curiosity as we did at them. Of the sermon, though delivered in a loud voice, we could understand nothing. I believe we understood as much as those who surrounded us, who were chiefly asleep. The whole ceremony lasted two hours. The Church itself is a fine specimen of the pointed style of architecture.

We spent the remainder of the day quietly in our

room untill dinner at five o'clock at the Table d'hôte, at which were eight french men and ourselves— greater nonsense or more determined gastronomy I never heard talked by reasonable people. We were as silent as they were talkative, and we gladly escaped to our rooms to prepare to walk in the environs of the town, which are charming. The Town itself, though small and dull, with narrow crooked streets, is a Prefecture.

We have observed in this part of Normandy the most magnificent Dogs that appear to us true mastiffs, and are probably so, introduced when this country was under English sway. On asking our landlord this evening what sort of dog they called them, he said they were of the kind called 'dogues'.

The climate here appears to us decidedly milder than in England; the autumn fruits are all ripe, even nuts, melons grow in the open air, double oleanders blossom freely at the cottage windows.

The dress of the peasantry is very picturesque. Today (Sunday) the men have mostly appeared in blue jackets and trowsers, with bright scarlet waistcoats. The high cap of the women is universal, but of various shapes and modifications. A very prevalent color in their dress is a brilliant rose color. They also wear short woolen peticoats striped of scarlet, green and black.

So far, we are delighted with Normandy. It is truly 'la belle Normandie'. 'Voila donc une grande perte pour vos rois, que la perte de la Normandie!' said our hostess of the 'Grand Turc' at Falaise.

At about ten, our usual hour, we parted to go to bed!

Monday August 13th, 1827
We set off directly after breakfast for Bayeux, where we arrived about twelve o'clock. The country was very sweet. We passed through the beautiful forest of Cerizy, where we understand wild boars are

Condé sur Noireau, KF

hunted and the breed encouraged for that purpose. They hunt them with the bulldogs (not mastifs) with which we were so much struck; they are sold at a very high price.

The people here call these fine animals 'dogues', which means bulldogs, I consider them mastiffs. Had I not been afraid of the trouble, I certainly should have bought a puppy to bring home. The wild boars are hunted on foot with rifles and spears; it is a sport I should much like to see.

The Norman horses deserve their high character. I think, next to our own, they are the best horses I have ever seen. They are strong, with a great deal of bone, but want a little more blood; they are by no means fast, but they can bear a great deal of fatigue. Like the horses and dogs, so the people are a very fine race; the men in particular are generally tall and well made. The picturesque dress of both men and women adds to their appearance. They seem to possess one valuable quality, the reverse of which I have generally found in France, viz. honesty.

The Inn here, 'the Hotel du Luxemburg', is pretty comfortable, a palace compared to Madame Nicholas' at Vire, though a few pounds of soap and a few scrubbing brushes, would add much to its good looks. I must say, I think the French are not extravagant in the use of these articles. The accumulated dirt and dust on the doors, windows and floors of many houses, would throw our clean housemaids into such a fever, that they never would recover, especially if they saw the gentlemen spitting all over the floors; I can't say on the carpets, for there are none. When the French understand a little better the meaning of our word 'comfortable', I think both carpets and cleanliness will be [introduced], in which case spitting *must* go out of fashion.

Bayeux

Immediately after our arrival here, we turned out to 'see the lions', first of which comes the famous Bayeux Tapestry, the most interesting object we have seen in Normandy. It is divided into fifty seven compartments, each one a representation of some particular event in the conquest of England by William the Conqueror, and each illusidated (for it would be difficult to tell without) by an explanatory latin inscription, in excellent intelligible Roman letters. It is about two feet deep. The ground work is white linen cloth and the figures are worked in worsteds of all colors, but so fancifully that the color of the horses' near and off legs different.

Where flesh was meant to be represented, we observed it was only worked in outline. There is no attempt at perspective, or light and shade. The costumes seem to be accurately kept to, but the figures are odd enough, and out of proportion, some men with very long legs, others with very short ones, and so on. It is kept with a good deal of care, on a large roller, though such frequent winding and unwinding must be injurious to such old materials. It is in wonderfully good repair considering its age, which is nearly eight centuries. This curious work is attributed by some to the Empress Maude, mother of King Stephen, but [by] the majority of others to (and by far the most probable) Maude, wife of King William the Conqueror.

The Cathedral of Bayeux is reconed the finest church in Normandy. It has two handsome square towers surmounted with lofty spires, and a noble dome that rivals them in hight. The architecture is mostly of the pointed style; the oldest part is said to have been built by that turbulent prelate, Bishop

North transept of choir,
Bayeux Cathedral, KF 1827

Odo, brother to William the Conqueror. It is in excellent repair, and kept clean and neat, but full of *wretched* paintings. On our way back to the hotel, the girls went into a shop and bought a true Norman cap, to astonish the natives at Plashet, and intended as a present for papa.

At four o'clock, we dined at the Table d'hôte. We found the company respectable and the dinner excellent; both boiled and roast meat were served up, with the former of which melon was eaten, to our surprise. Both yesterday and to day we have been amused in seeing the arrival, departure, loading and unloading of sundry Diligences; one rumbled into the Inn yard at St Lo, drawn by *nine* horses. It carried between twenty and thirty passengers in and upon it. Of this wagon-looking thing, K. made a sketch.

After dinner, we went again to the Cathedral, and after walking a little about the town went home to our Café. The evening was spent as usual in drawing and writing.

The next morning, about eleven o'clock, we set off for our old quarters at Caen. The country through which we passed was flat and uninteresting, but highly cultivated.

After our arrival at Caen we set off to call on the Abbotts and bought some little trinkets on our way. As we came home, we were struck by the beauty and variety of the flowers in the market. We bought some that were new to us, and if they can bear so long a journey, we mean to give them to mamma. We understand that the reason they were there to day in

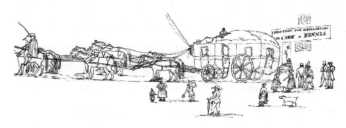

Diligence carrying 18 inside passengers and six outside.
Inn yard, St Lo, KF 1827

such variety is that tomorrow is the fête of the Virgin, and flowers are considered the most elegant present that can be given on such an occasion.

We dined at the Table d'hôte with a large but respectable party, and in the evening the Abbotts and Mrs Sherwell called on us, to fix tomorrow's plans. Monsieur Pelletier also called but we were out. Katharine and I quietly settled to our occupations, whilst William went to return his call, but unluckily he was not at home.

Tuesday August 14th, 1827

After breakfast we settled quietly till eleven o'clock. The town this morning is very gay, no work is done, the shops are closed and all the people in their best attire are thronging to the Churches, for it is 'le jour du fête de la sainte vierge'. Our friends all assembled here, the Abbotts, Sherwells, and Monsieur Pelletier. We first went to Saint Etienne, the ancient church of the 'Abbaye aux Hommes', built by William the Conqueror, where fully twenty ecclesiastics in the most gorgeous costumes were saying mass. They wore copes of gold embroidery, lace, &ca. The music was lovely, and the whole scene most imposing.

We then went [to] the Lycée, a large public school which now occupies the ancient 'Abbaye aux hommes' built by King William the Conqueror, in which till the Revolution resided thirty monks and sixty servants. The inlaid floors, now rough with the trampling of boys' feet, its carved ceilings and frescoed walls, the long coridors and spacious halls give an idea that these reverend fathers were not particularly self denying in their private lives. Its present application is one of much greater public utility: several hundred boys, the sons of gentlemen, receive there a good education. One wing is given up to lectures and school-rooms, where the scholars receive the instruction of masters; the different classes then prepare their tasks in several smaller schoolrooms, under the care of an usher. The great boys eat in one hall, the little ones in another. The sleeping is admirably contrived: immense coridors, lofty and light, are divided by wooden partitions into little compartments, each of which contains a bed, table, chair, looking glass, washhandstand, &ca. They are open at top to admit of the free circulation of the air, and in front is trellis work, so that all that passes within can be seen. A master sleeps at each end of the apartment, in a similar compartment, only larger and better; the boys are locked in and cannot communicate; the Masters see and hear every thing. About 100 boys are in each room. A watchman with a light is up all night walking about the rooms to see that all is safe and right. The boys are taught, fed and lodged. The education consists of the classics, history, geography, philosophy, arethmetic, geometry, algebra, trigonometry, statistics, natural history, mineralogy, chimistry, physic, astronomy, English, drawing &ca, and all this for 700 francs a year.

After this we went into many of the churches, all decorated with flowers for the fête of the Virgin. Also, leaving Chenda at the hotel, we visited a curious old house in the suberbs that is mentioned in the Abbé de la Rue's history of Caen, and in Dawson Turner's Normandy.

Monsieur Pellitier dined with us at our hotel; dinner was served in my bedroom, quite à la française—my room is our living room and a great deal of company has been received in it. After dinner our English friends joined us and we went to the 'Hopital de St Louis', a delightful institution for Enfans Trouvés.

William now writes: We were met at the Gate by the Lady Abbess, who is a very pretty, nice looking, rather young woman. The ladies of our party expressed great delight at the sight of a number of little infants only a few days old, just taken in, all lying in a row of pretty little cribs, perhaps fifteen or twenty, attended with great kindness and attention by three or four old nurses, superintended by a nun. I thought the poor little babies' legs were swaddled up unnaturally tight. In a large room adjoining we saw 40 to 50 little things from three to six years old asleep in bed, and further on a number a little older were at play. Besides these, there are several hundred young children out at nurse with respectable poor people in the country. The boys are brought up and educated for soldiers.

Adjoining to this institution and superintended by the same nuns is an Hospital, institution into which are admitted decrepid old people of all sorts, people who have any incurable desease upon them, besides a few crazy people and idiots. Though not in such fine order, or quite so well managed as the Abbé aux Dames, it is still a fine institution.

Katharine now takes the pen. In relating the history of this day, we have most strangely omitted to mention the most remarkable feature in it: our visit to the Town

Gaol, an admission into the interior of which, given by the Mayor, was a favor scarcely ever known to have been granted before. Like every thing else in France, a military guard was placed over it. We entered by a little low door, into a dark, gloomy sort of passage, through which we literally groaped to the kitchen inhabited by the governor and his family. The construction of the prison was on this plan. The governor's house

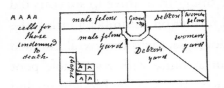

is intended to inspect the yards but even this object is defeated by his residence on the ground floor, and *letting* the other rooms to the deptors.

There is no distinction between the tried and untried prisoners, and the windows of the debtors entirely command the women's yard. No matron or female officers. The debtors sleep on beds, for which they pay. The felons have only straw and the effect of their rooms was rather miserable, and to our English eyes, dirty. The Untried are not compelled to work, those who have received sentence are obliged to work, but being jour de fête we saw nothing of it. They hear

117

mass on Sundays, and jours de fête. The effect of the women was tollerable, the men were remarkably ill looking. The most sad and objectionable things we saw were the cells for those condemned to death, in which they are kept sometimes as long as six weeks; they are dark, light and air only admitted through a grated hole communicating with a dismal passage. The general effect of the Prison was an intention to do well by the prisoners, but a total ignorance of the simplist principles of Prison Discipline. We concluded this fatiguing day by spending the evening at our kind friend Mrs Sherwell's.

Wednesday August 15th, 1827
This day at eleven o'clock our day's work began. Our French and English friends assembled and we went off together to the great central prison of the surrounding Department called Bicêtre or Beaulieu, about a mile distant from this town. Monsieur Martin drove three of the ladies in his cabriolet, the rest walked.

On first arriving we waited some time in the guard room, and were then ushered into the presence of the Governor. In every thing in this country there is a sort of assumption of official importance that infinitely amuses me. The Governor, however, was very civil and harangued us at full length on the subject of Prison Discipline, which it seems is just now claiming great attention in France. They have in the Kingdom twenty of these central prisons, 'maisons centrale', in which those who are sentenced to more than one year's imprisonment are confined. They are all employed and paid one third of their earnings at the time, one third on leaving the prison; the other third goes to the government and forms at Paris a fund that accumulates, and it is calculated will in fifty years amount to a sum the interest of which will be sufficient to defray the expences of the Prison, aided by the earnings of the prisoners, who are now an expence of 10 sous, 5d English each, daily to the government. Since the introduction of labour, many reformations among the less hardened cases have occured. The returns about twenty in a hundred.

This harangue ceasing, we took our leave with many thanks, and attended by a soldier went round the Prison, a sensible well behaved man, and I must confess with manners very superior to his rank in life. All the taskmasters, turnkeys, &ca, were military. I asked him the reason. 'Mais oui mademoiselle, nous faisons tout en France à la militaire; en Angleterre on me dit, que ce n'est pas comme ça.' 'Non Monsieur, chez nous les militaries ne se mellent jamais des affairs civiles.'

The prisoners, seven hundred in number, of whom two hundred and eighty are women, are all employed; they are classed not according to crime, but to trade, each being employed in his own trade, carpenters, makers of Sabots, weavers, cotton spinners, &ca, all sorts of machinery. Those who know no trade are taught one.

The women have a yard to themselves, but the seperation between them and the men is by no means complete. They are employed in lace making, embroidery, and plain work, which they do beautifully. In every ward was stationed a soldier, who acts as taskmaster, and inspector. The prisoners appeared to stand greatly in awe of these men, who we were told are allowed to strike them.

The infirmary looked clean and comfortable, with only eight or ten sick in it; they say they seldom have more. The prison allowance of food is soup and bread daily, but they are allowed to purchase meat and other indulgences for themselves. Some of the male prisoners were cooks, the kitchen small but sufficient. Each ward had a wardsman, or woman, selected from among the Prisoners, who receiving a small salery and having other priviledges it is an object of emulation and is given to the best behaved. There is a Prison dress, good and suitable, beds and bedding very sufficient, large dormitaries, ninety in a room; a guard passes through hourly. They hear mass on Sundays and fête days. The general effect of the prison quiet & orderly. The *faults* are the construction of the prison, which prevents the constant, and unknown, inspection of the Governor himself, the want of classification according to crime, and of female officers for the women. The prisoners have no recreation but half an hour for breakfast, one hour for dinner, and half [an] hour for supper.

Returning from Bicêtre, I was put in the Cabriolet, but it was frightful. Lumps, holes, heaps of stones were all the same to our agreeable and chatty french companion and his good natured horse. On we went —the reins under his tail nearly caused us to upset into a ditch, but did not suspend the conversation of our friend. We went to the Saint Sauveur Convent, where is a very delightful deaf and dumb school. Also an immense establishment for insane persons of all ranks, under the care of the Sisters.

We returned to our hotel almost anihilated with fatigue, dined at the Table d'hôte as usual, and intending to start at five the next morning for Evreux, we went in the evening to call and take leave of our friends. At the Abbotts, Chenda, who was a good deal knocked up and indeed had never been well the whole journey, was seized with violent pain and sickness, and it was with difficulty we got her home to the hotel.

I was up with her almost all the night, and in the morning, the complaint not having at all abated, we thought it right to send for Dr Kelly, an Irish pract[it]ioner here. He came, gave her some medicine and promised to return in two hours, desiring William not to confine himself here, as there was not the least cause for alarm. Mrs Sherwell and Mrs Abbott came to spend the day with us, and William and Mr Abbott went to La Deliverande.

About one o'clock Dr Kelly returned. Her agonies of pain were affecting to witness and he pronounced it 'active inflammation of the bowels' and progressing fast, for which it was necessary to bleed her copiously immediately. I was already greatly alarmed and this information brought me into a conflict of mind that is more easily to be imagined than described. Alone, among strangers, though kind and friendly strangers, in a foreign town, with that poor child under my care (age about 18) raving in a sort of hysterical dilirium. He said her life was at stake. I of course consented, but first walked up and down the room (next hers) in a degree of distress that is not to be imagined. Dr Kelly banished me her room whilst he bled her. I ran messages from very nervousness. I felt as though it was quite impossible to give her up, even to dangerous illness. I thought of home, of our parents, of the strength of a many times twisted cord at such moments, and then the sensation of my lonely desolate situation came over me like an oppressive cloud. I was standing thus in the Hotel Yard, feeling so entirely alone, when it came over me that a Good and Benevolent Providence was overruling all these events, that death must come upon us all, and that whether it took place in a foreign land or not little mattered, provided it was in His own time, and ordered by His will. I felt the conflict over and going upstairs I wept, greatly to my own relief.

Dr Kelly thought my alarm unreasonable; he was rough with me and assured me with vehement protestations that there was no cause for alarm, which to my other pains added that of want of confidence in the doctor. William came home at 5 o'clock. The sight of the street littered down with straw made his heart sink within him. She was too ill to be allowed to see him. Our English friends kept with us, with the affection and sympathy that is invaluable at such moments. Our two french acquaintance (the medical students Pelletier and Martin), they earnestly desired to see Dr Kelly, which he refused, even though we begged it; he would neither meet them nor speak to them.

Mrs Sherwell sat up with her and we hired a nurse to attend her, as we had no maid. I lay down but did not sleep. The next day we moved her into my room, which is larger than hers, and more airy. She was allowed to see no one but Mrs Abbott and Mrs Sherwell, and I was still banished her room; such was her state of weakness and nervous irritation that she could not bear to see me. This day was one of the most painful I ever passed!

Mrs Sherwell again sat up with her and I was put

into a strange room upstairs, where I again lay all night sleepless.

Sunday August 19th, 1827
This day, no return of the complaint gave us hope and William went to Guibray with Mr Abbott. Mrs Sherwell and I dined at the Table d'hôte. The enquiries after Chenda were kind and polite. There is a certain polish and urbanity in the external manners of the french, which is to me extremely pleasing, and I cannot help feeling myself more at ease with them than with my countrymen.

Monday August 20th, 1827
We continue to go on just the same. We got her out of bed, to have it made, but she nearly fainted with the exertion, and we were glad to get her back into it.

Dr Kelly comes five or six times a day, giving always the most violent medecines and staying three quarters of an hour at a time. I begin to dislike his practice very much; he is always promising what an alteration we shall see Tomorrow. He has allowed her this day to eat.

125

Tuesday August 21st, 1827

Nothing but a repetition of the old thing, no return of strength, still violent medecines. Our friends, as well as William and myself, much discontented. More medecine at night, which was restless and full of pain.

Wednesday August 22nd, 1827

This morning I gently told Dr Kelly that I saw no return of strength, and that not being in the habit of taking violent medecines at home, I was a little afraid of the present system. On seeing her, he declared all medecine was now unnecessary, that she was recovering rapidly, and that we might certainly travel on Monday next. We got her out of bed onto some easy chairs for a few hours. She saw our french friends this evening. They have all along been uneasy at her treatment. Her doctor paid us a short visit, and confirming the report of the morning went away. She passed a good night, and in the morning seemed charmingly. I went upstairs to breakfast in William's room, but returning in about half an hour, found her hurried, agitated, feverish and in pain. Dr Kelly had been with her. Told her he saw that I was dissatisfied with his treatment of her, and that he should therefore not return unless I sent for him. That she ought to take more medecine, but that he should leave the responsibility on my shoulders, that she was very liable to relapses, and indeed would have one immediately, and in short frightened her extremely. William and I were much displeased. I went off immediately to our friends (Mr and Mrs Abbott and Mrs Sherwell) and all agreed that we had better send him a fee and let him go. I therefore wrote him a short note, begging his acceptance of a hundred & twenty francs (£5).

Messieurs Pelletier and Martin came to us. They assured us there was no return or symptom of return of her complaint. I omitted to say that the Doctor in his extraordinary visit this morning told Chenda that it would be very dangerous to move her on Monday, but that he dare not say so to me, I seemed so determined to go. For the satisfaction of us all, we agreed to call in Monsieur Trouvée, the principal French Physician in Caen, a man of great skill and reputation. He could not come before the evening, and Pelletier and Martin took upon themselves to allow her to go out in the carriage. They assisted William to carry her down, and then Monsieur Pelletier accompanied the carriage on foot, Mrs Sherwell inside with her, and William on the box. The procession moved slowly onto the 'grand cours', a fine drive and walk by the side of the river Orne, a sort of Boulvard. She stayed out nearly half an hour, and returned so extremely fatigued that she was carried nearly fainting to her bed. We undressed her and put her into it, when she fell asleep, and awoke her for her dinner, which she eat with appetite and found herself really revived.

In the Evening we again got her into an easy chair for an hour or two. But she received M. Trouvée, her new doctor, in bed. He said he could not judge of her real state in one visit but was very encouraging, ordered her cooling drinks for the night and a linseed poultice, which Messrs Pelletier and Martin made up most skillfully for her, which has wonderfully relieved the soreness and pain in her stomach and side. The Irish doctor's absence is a wonderful relief.

Thursday August 30th, 1827

Many days have now elapsed since I last wrote. Our invalid has gone on perfectly well under the care of the French physician, with our kind young doctors for his aids de camps. She is now dressed, drives out daily, eats with an apetite, and has all other symptoms of recovery. Our evenings have been the most bright spots in our lives here, and they become brighter and brighter as they are more near ceasing for ever. All our friends regularly spend them with us. Coffee and syrops are our refreshment whilst singing, and Monsieur Pelletier's guitar, together with poetry, conversation, and that inexpressible charm that accompanies the unrestrained intercourse of friends, linked together on the one side by the truest kindness and desire to render happy, and on the other by gratitude.

On Tuesday, William and Mr Abbott went off for England. I dreaded William's departure very much indeed and felt so much responsibility would devolve on me, together with a little question as to the propriety of our being left alone in a foreign country at an hotel. However, circumstances

Church of Notre Dame, Caen, KF 1827

have dispersed this cloud also. Lord and Lady St Vincent, now at this hotel, desire us to consider them as our protectors, and I have twice been out in the town with them, to show them the lions of the place. Chenda is so much better and our friends are so good in coming that we have no sense of loneliness.

On Tuesday 28th I went with Mrs Sherwell, Lady St Vincent and her daughter to witness the ceremony of taking the White Veil at the convent of the Hospital of St Louis in this town. We were placed on chairs on the steps of the alter. The ceremony commenced by saying mass. The young woman, a pleasing looking person, of about twenty five years of age, was remarkably calm and collected during the whole ceremony. She was seated on a chair within the 'Grille' but when she advanced to the door we saw her distinctly. The priests then with great form and marshalling went to the door of the Grille, and asked her in french whether she renounced the world willingly, to which she replied with a firm voice, 'Oui mon père.' Then an old priest mounted the pulpit and preached us an excellent and interesting sermon, on the love of God to man, and on the blessings that flowed directly from him. The especial advantage of having pious parents was dwelt on, which it seemed this young woman had possessed in no common degree. It was to me quite affecting. The sermon, which was long, having ceased, the singing of the mass recommenced, the dress she had to wear was blessed, she was taken out and clothed in them, came in to the church again, and after a good deal of chanting, kneeling, bowing, &ca, the ceremony concluded.

The next day, with the permission of the nuns, we took Lord and Lady St Vincent to visit the Convent, and the charitable institutions attached to it, with which they were much gratified, and two days [later] I conducted them to the Abbaye aux Dames, over which Monsieur Pelletier showed us. It loses no interest in a second visit; in fact it was far more interesting the second than the first time, and being sociable with Pelletier we could ask questions and really saw more than on our first visit.

Chenda is going on well and almost looks like herself once more. Mrs Sherwell is with us daily two or even three times and is the greatest pleasure and comfort to us, as well as her sweet and amiable children. We miss William surprisingly little and though alone, we cannot be said to be unprotected.

Saturday September 1st, 1827

Chenda went to the Sherwells to take leave, and Lord and Lady St Vincent hapening to come in, she got quite overcome and hysterical. I was forced to go home alone to the Hotel for dinner and send a carriage up for her.

Pelletier came early to speak about his friend Monsieur Ameline, now in London. She could not bear to hear us talk. I therefore went with him onto the Cours. This day Monsieur Martin spent with us: he came from the country on purpose to take leave of us, and surprised us by his appearance the evening before, whilst we were at Coffee. He took his leave at night, as he was going to Paris at five o'clock the next morning.

Sunday September 2nd, 1827

This was the last day of our very interesting residence at Caen. Pelletier breakfasted with us and Monsieur Trouvée came after breakfast, when I had a full explanation respecting Chenda's illness, its probable causes and the future treatment of her.

After that we got a little on with packing, and then went to dine with Mrs Abbott, after receiving Lord and Lady St Vincent to take leave. Then we returned to our hotel and had one more pleasant evening with the Sherwells and Monsieur Pelletier, but clouded with the recollection that it was the *last*. Monsieur P. took leave of us that evening.

But on the 3rd Mrs Sherwell and her dear children were with us by seven o'clock. Parting with the Sherwells was very painful to us, and we drove silent and thoughtful out of Caen, a place frought with most interesting recollections for us, and one which I shall never forget.

Our journey to Honfleur was altogether prosperous. We had one little contretemps from a kicking horse, who got himself so entangled as to detain us nearly half an hour, and give me serious fears of some injury to the carriage, which was however prevented.

At Honfleur we went to the Hotel d'Espagne, far better than the Hotel d'Angleterre to us, now that we are cured of our hankerings after the least fag end of an Englishman.

We found the Havre packet would not come till evening, so having laid Chenda down on a bed, I seated myself at a window whilst waiting for dinner to read. But the interesting view that it commanded and the reflections it induced soon diverted me from my book.

The little port of Honfleur, divided by little piers into three basins with sloops and fishing smacks, the wooded hights above the town to the right, and the winding Seine losing itself at length among the distant hills, Havre opposite, with its fine port and forts, and backed by the 'Côté St Michael', just to be distinguished and on the left of the Ocean. It was a rare combination of bold grandeur, picturesque beauty and rich populous scenery. I thought with real regret of being about to quit these lovely scenes half explored and half enjoyed, perhaps never to see them again; and then turning to the sea, I could not but feel it rather an undertaking to cross that expance of water with so delicate an invalid as Chenda—and as twilight advanced and the sun was setting, the clear, bright looking town of Havre beginning to dim in the distance, until only a few straggling lights marked where it was, the evening breeze to rise, and the tide which was gradually filling the Harbour, breaking over the bar, and rolling all the craft that lay before so still upon the mud, I could not [but] anxiously watch for the approaching steamer that was to convey us across. Even a good dinner, generally so attractive to hungry and exhausted travellers, could not prevent my constantly looking towards Havre, in the anxious hope of seeing the smoke of our steamer. At this moment our travelling servant Nicholas announced 'un Monsieur anglais', who requested permission to wait on us, and after the proper preliminaries of a card, &ca, it proved to be Thomas Christy junior. He was going across to Le Havre and of course offered us his escort, which we gladly accepted.

At length the steam packet came and maneuvered into the basin. I immediately ordered the carriage to be shipped, but [to] my great disappointment, on taking poor Chenda down to the pier, there stood the carriage! and the Captain refused to take it on board because the sea breaking over the bar tossed the packet a good deal, and it was now dark. Chenda went off into a great agitation and there we were, the french sailors chattering to me about the impracticability of getting the carriage on board, and Thomas Christy and our own servant Nicholas both lost!

At length they came, and getting Chenda on board with some difficulty, also a few needful packages from the carriage, we were obliged to leave it and Nicholas at

Honfleur—very glad to have a gentleman to escort us.

I felt almost as glad when I entered the harbour of Le Havre this second time as when we felt ourselves out of our miseries on passing its forts and entrance the first time. Captain Brice of the St David had engaged rooms for us at the hotel du 'Bien Venue', where we were very comfortable. Chenda had borne the exertions of this very full day tollerably well and I felt no doubt of getting her home safe, although I was fully aware that it was no light undertaking, and that could we have done so with propriety, a week or two more rest would have been of great advantage to her.

Tuesday September 4th, 1827

This was a flat day of a sort of busy idleness. The carriage came over from Honfleur; it passed the Custom House, as well as our luggage previous to embarkation. We also got our passeports visée, and the permission for our embarkation, &ca, &ca, and eight o'clock in the evening, we once more put out to Sea in the St David, with about fifty passengers, and ten horses, in little stables on the deck.

It was perfectly smooth at first, not wind enough even to carry off our smoke. But in about an hour, when we got quite out to sea, we found a good deal of sea on, which came upon our beams, and made the vessel roll a good deal; also continual and heavy squalls of wind and rain from the northeast. The poor horses were sadly frightened and kicked a great deal, disturbing every body with their noise. Poor Chenda was wretchedly ill; she and I had a little cabin to ourselves. The vessel was almost as much as when crossed before, for the seas took her in so different a position, that although there was no comparison as to the violence of the sea, it was almost as disagreeable to be on it.

I had a fatiguing night's nursing. Every now and then I went for a moment on deck to see the Sea: it was a fine sight, a bright moon reflected on the wild dark waters, and the yet wilder sky, with the black squally clouds casting their shaddows on the sea. About three in the morning, it settled into a steady, brisk breeze, which made the air very cold, but enabled us to carry a little sail, and we went comparatively steadily through the water.

Chenda fell asleep and the Captain advised me to creep into the berth under hers, where I fell fast asleep, and when I woke found the sun shining through the little cabin window. Chenda had been again very ill, but the Captain had waited on her. It was about six o'clock. We did not, however, get into water smooth enough for breakfast to be served till between twelve & one o'clock. About eleven, Chenda was got onto the poop deck. The Isle of Wight was in full view—very beautiful! At three o'clock we entered the Southampton water and soon observed in a little boat scudding along by our side our cousin Richard Fry, come, he said, to accompany us home.

Very thankful indeed did I feel when I saw Chenda laying quietly asleep on the sofa at the Star Inn at Southampton, to think she was on this side the Channel. But our voyage had sadly thrown her back and we did not reach Plashet till the 7th of the month. We found dearest mamma in Norfolk, a great disappointment, and Chenda is certainly thrown back many degrees.

Postscript

There is an explanation for Richenda's emotional outbursts in Caen—and perhaps even for her illness. It comes to light in a letter from Katharine to their mother, written shortly after their return to England:

About Chenda and Monsieur M., I told Lucy Sherwell at Caen, and now repeat it, that I do not consider Chenda old enough, or mature enough, to be allowed to take so serious a step as to marry a Roman Catholic, and a foreigner.

Like Captain Brice's attachment, this romance is not even hinted at in the diary but is confirmed many years later in the Family Record. After giving a brief account of the holiday, Katharine wrote: 'Very shortly after our return home, a formal offer of marriage was made to our parents from a French man of good family and estate in Normandy.'

There is no record of what Richenda felt about Captain Brice but it seems likely, from her volatile state and the wording of Katharine's letter, that she had fallen in love with Monsieur M. and that Katharine, taking her position *in loco parentis* very seriously, had vetoed the attachment. No wonder Richenda was hysterical.

However, she was not inconsolable for long. The following spring, when Katharine was staying with her sister Rachel, their mother wrote to tell them of Richenda's engagement to Foster Reynolds. Richenda's enclosed note shows that she held no grudge against her eldest sister:

> *Write to me most fully my dearest, dearest sisters,*
> *I long to hear from you and see you! Pray do send*
> *Katharine home. I have great support, and hope I*
> *am thankful, but I want hers also.*

Richenda was married in June 1828, with Katharine as bridesmaid, and there was a large, happy family party at Plashet. It was almost the last. Katharine remarked: 'How little did we think that before the year 1828 had closed we should be as outcasts from that happy home!!!' The family banking house crashed, largely, according to the Family Record, as a result of their uncle William's speculations in South American mines, and the tea business run by Joseph was inextricably enmeshed in the crisis.

Plashet was put up for sale and the family was forced to find somewhere more modest. In October 1829, they moved to their new house in Upton Lane, West Ham. Katharine mourned the change.

It was indeed a deeply affecting realization of our changed circumstances ... the house and offices are not commodious; it is very damp and the want of any garden makes it very confined. Our household is composed of Chrissy (Golder) and Sarah Atherton, a cook and a housemaid; much personal superintendence is required from me, and even some cooking.

But, in less than two years, she was able to report 'much cheerfulness and enjoyment' at the new house. It was eventually improved and enlarged, and 'the little square garden grew into one of singular variety and charm, although small, laid out by our father's most skillful hand.' They were also shown great kindness by Sir Henry and Lady Pelly of Upton Park, who 'received us warmly and opened their grounds to us in the summer evenings'.

At the time of the move, seven of Elizabeth and Joseph's children were still living at home. William, who became a partner in the tea business when it was salvaged from the bankruptcy by Elizabeth's brothers, was amongst them. In 1832, he married Juliana Pelly in Upton and, after two years at St Mildred's Court, settled down at the nearby Manor House. Less than three years later, his youngest sister, Louisa, became the wife of Juliana's brother Raymond.

William was married for just twelve years. In 1844, shortly after he returned home from settling his parents and Katharine in a house by the sea for the summer, his daughter was taken seriously ill.

We had only passed nine quiet days at Walmer when the post brought us the sorrowful news of the death of ... our beloved brother William's second girl, Juliana Katharine in the seventh year of her age... the complaint was supposed to be suppressed scarlet fever falling on the brain ... Our beloved brother himself appeared greatly upset by the event and was very sick, which was called nervous. His wife was preserved in much calmness but in a state near her confinement, unable to move about or make any exertion.

William, too ill to attend his small daughter's funeral, asked that his bedroom door should be left open so he could see her coffin being carried downstairs. He died shortly afterwards and was buried in the same grave. Three days later another daughter, Emma, joined them. Two more of his seven children were taken ill but recovered. Katharine pasted a silhouette of William, done at the time of his wedding, into the Family Record: 'As no really good picture remains of our dear brother we insert this imperfect shadow. He died before photography was discovered.'

Of Richenda's five children, two died before reaching adulthood. One daughter accomplished what her mother had been prevented from doing thirty years earlier: in November 1857 Esther Marianne Reynolds married a Frenchman, Hippolyte Louis Antonio d'Arbour of Caen. It is not clear how successful the marriage was, but Katharine, revisiting Normandy in 1865, implies that all was not well: 'The first interest in this place was poor Marianne Darbour and her family.' Richenda, now a widow, was also living nearby at the time.

Chenda's ménage here is, according to our ideas, exceedingly droll. We approach the cottage from the road by means of a wicket gate, through a rough garden, composed of quitch grass and tamarisk, perhaps I might rather say up a steep bank as there are two flights of steps of wood before arriving on the platform where stands the cottage nestled in shrubs.

When Elizabeth Fry, having been ill for some time, died in 1845, Joseph gave up the house in Upton Lane and moved with Katharine to Plashet Cottage in the grounds of their old home. She took care of him until his death sixteen years later.

It was August of this year 1861 that our father's long life of eighty-four years was brought to its close. He had for two years been in a state of such infirmity as to render it needful for him to be sat up with at night, as he was often terribly agitated, not knowing where he was or who were with him ... On 5th September we laid him in the same grave as our beloved mother in the Burying Ground of Friends at Barking. It was a quiet, private funeral, attended by his children and grandchildren and many of our cousins.

Joseph left Katharine the cottage at Plashet for her lifetime. She lived there for another twenty-five years, wrapped up in the concerns of her brothers and sisters, nieces and nephews. Between 1870 and

1880, with the help of her youngest brother Daniel, she worked on the Family Record, a history of the family of which she was a part for so long. Into the big leather-bound volume, as well as her researches into the Fry and Gurney histories, she copied a great quantity of letters, not only from family members but also from the great and the good, who corresponded with her mother.

Katharine closed her long account with a nostalgic look back at happy days with the Pelly family in the 1830s. By a quirk of fate, the Beacontree archery club near Leytonstone, where they had spent many hours together, was now a Friends Meeting House. There, she observed, 'in the old archery ground, now the burying ground of the Society of Friends, are interred some very dear to us.' Richenda was buried there in 1884 and there, too, according to a note (probably by Daniel) in the Family Record

on 13 May 1886 Katharine Fry,
the compiler of this book, was laid to her rest.

Index

148

If you have enjoyed this book, you may also be interested in

Miss Brocklehurst on the Nile
(diary of a Victorian Traveller in Egypt)

For information on this or any other Millrace title, please get in touch, or have a look at our website:

www.millracebooks.co.uk

Millrace
2a Leafield Road
Disley, Cheshire SK12 2JF
tel: + 44 (0)1663 765080